The Daily Telegraph

Cryptic Crossword Book
54

Also available in Pan Books

and in Macmillan

and for more titles visit www.panmacmillan.com

The Daily Telegraph
Cryptic Crossword Book
54

Pan Books
in association with *The Daily Telegraph*

First published in 2005 by Pan Books

This edition first published 2018 by Pan Books
an imprint of Pan Macmillan, a division of Macmillan Publishers Limited
Pan Macmillan, 20 New Wharf Road, London N1 9RR
Associated companies throughout the world
www.panmacmillan.com

In association with *The Daily Telegraph*

ISBN 978-1-509-89384-3

A CIP catalogue record for this book is available from the
British Library.

Visit **www.panmacmillan.com** to read more about all our books and to buy
them. You will also find features, author interviews and news of any author
events, and you can sign up for e-newsletters so that you're always first to hear
about our new releases.

ACROSS

1 Boldness to surface in confrontation (4,2,4)
6 Quiet drink in exclusive district (4)
9 Tom, we learn, stewed fruit (5-5)
10 Minor ailment heard of in Chile (4)
13 Some vermin are trapped in tower (7)
15 False denial pinned down (6)
16 Beam – one's offered support at high level (6)
17 Don't use this lever? Nonsense! (4,3,5,3)
18 Soldiers' inclination to be prompt (6)
20 Angler – she is in tree (6)
21 Stick a leg back with can of glue (7)
22 Loved ancient portion of scripture (4)
25 Devious stratagem, I judge (10)
26 Flooring lion, twisting its tail (4)
27 Mint coin for the king (10)

DOWN

1 Cringe as wife has admirer round (4)
2 Sweet slice eaten to start with (4)
3 Hot and clear below peak (6)
4 Cafeteria is soon bubbling with a flow of words (4,11)
5 Life of luxury among such plants (6)
7 Raised mark where something was dropped, perhaps (10)
8 Fruit unsuitable for younger people? (10)
11 Awaiting judgment – not needing to pay yet (2,8)
12 Foolish fellow crossing motorway for place in field (5,3-2)
13 Satisfying get-together (7)
14 Understood one's been tricked (5,2)
19 Lower to seabed somehow (6)
20 More suitable as assemblyman? (6)

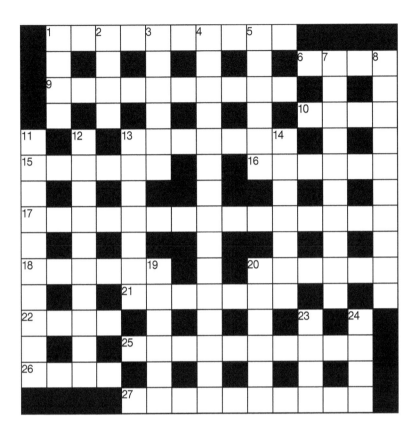

23 It patrols the ocean blue (4)
24 Some film making one stagger (4)

ACROSS

1 One elects to put a cross on it (6-5)
9 Moved a deer and colt and put them in different places (9)
10 A practitioner goes round hospital for this special purpose (2,3)
11 Had a teasing desire – then scratched? (6)
12 Taxes one, one North of the Border (8)
13 Financial return (6)
15 It in the convent is of first importance (8)
18 Marge's so embarrassed by the very thin material (8)
19 Leonard back behind marsh plant (6)
21 Impetus for a second before hesitation in speech (8)
23 Scare rebel leader in combat (6)
26 Ruler? (5)
27 Loquacious lecture at teatime perhaps by expedition leader (9)
28 Time to retire – eventually (3,2,3,3)

DOWN

1 Author runs under fence (7)
2 Piccalilli lacked some colour (5)
3 Carthorse startled musicians (9)
4 Course taken by a non-driver? (4)
5 Corny treatment? (8)
6 It ran around laughing (5)
7 Carriage from part of the East End (7)
8 Defend top dog (8)
14 Where one goes down for bargains (8)
16 Extend beyond Andover reaching the interior (9)
17 However their leader in a rush was disproved (8)
18 Get away with Jim first reportedly in a tunic (7)
20 Supply (7)

22 Never-changing audacity (5)
24 It is hard work to turn the crank (5)
25 Almost split the key (4)

ACROSS

1 One-time player – such a demanding guy! (7)
5 Get the small child more suitable reading-matter (7)
9 The shifty grandee caused exasperation (7)
10 Calling for the waterproofing of footwear (7)
11 It could be apt in time to appear irritable (9)
12 Turner put many articles together (5)
13 A canvas support (5)
15 Back the head's strict attitude (9)
17 Journalists divided about incontestable obligations (9)
19 Keen to take silver in always (5)
22 Viewed, so it's said, as disagreement (5)
23 Count the money with grim consequences (9)
25 To charm some women a mournful look is best (7)
26 Fancy a copy with lining in (7)
27 Spirit creates respect (7)
28 People putting up with others (7)

DOWN

1 Solitary before time changed him (7)
2 Meet a sailor going around the shore (7)
3 Not relaxed, having drunk rather too much (5)
4 He will set one right concerning kitchen furniture (9)
5 A youngster undergoing training acted badly (5)
6 Transport the general public aren't fit to use (9)
7 First trainee taken into the plant (7)
8 Back up rebel leader, way-out (7)
14 A yobbo must accept a woman's attacks (6,3)
16 Making a list seen as vital (9)
17 Have to get the sheriff's men onto a ship (7)
18 Offer a lift (7)
20 Tearing about to find a certain type of stone (7)
21 Joints where jackets are required (7)

23 A service held by the French in Ulster (5)
24 A king, and so majestic (5)

ACROSS

1 Simmer with emotion and give a little cry, offered leftovers? (6,3,6)
9 Entertain with port (7)
10 Twin cats? (7)
11 Man placed in line-out (4)
12 Act, but wrong to be unsure (5)
13 Some dress – a rich Indian wears it (4)
16 Muster for duty to clear lumber (4,3)
17 Useful fund could be within one's clutch (4,3)
18 Time passes so, as sleep is problematic (7)
21 Almost demonstrate one's old condition (7)
23 Squint at performers (4)
24 Rudely brief, securing love to woo (5)
25 Second child has a slide (4)
28 Casual dress 11 messed up with egg (7)
29 Chime popular with one opera composer (7)
30 Hopeful gets into trouble with spoken blunder (4,2,3,6)

DOWN

1 Responsible for tantrums out of public view? (6,3,6)
2 Scottish playwright runs into block (7)
3 Student returns low mill machine (4)
4 Bearing left for Luton, say (7)
5 Refuse to enter this collectors' item (7)
6 Landing place sounds important (4)
7 Leave out note for lift (7)
8 Guarding merry-making, as watch should be? (7,4,4)
14 Promote sale initially in appropriate part of car (5)
15 Charm initially unwanted for race meeting (5)
19 Fool, for example, over excellent weapon (7)
20 Drunkard one's interrupted very quickly (7)

21 eg Sower quietly going over ploughed land (7)
22 Some idea that sepia has connection with fish (7)
26 King converted oil to metric quantity (4)
27 He may have some ethereal top notes (4)

ACROSS

1 Registered refusal to make hay (5)
4 Brisk beating (8)
10 Boil has to be treated to put an end to it (7)
11 Having trouble getting a piston replaced (2,1,4)
12 Pronouncement made by a servant (4)
13 Way to rebuke and administer corporal punishment (5)
14 Useless to be cocky (4)
17 A paper's emblem is indicative of today (4,2,3,5)
19 Recover personal-property and settle scores (3,4,3,4)
22 Outline a scheme (4)
23 Common vegetables used to make Sunday desserts (5)
24 Eager to acquire knowledge about the Orient (4)
27 Where to find a woman after Pentecost? (7)
28 Regards mineral deposit as a blemish (7)
29 I may tend to become explosive (8)
30 Brush up on the lottery (5)

DOWN

1 Lucky escape from the girl next door (4,4)
2 Motorists' warning to pedestrians in London (7)
3 Murder a Spanish nobleman without one (2,2)
5 His CO may order: "Deliver to Paris" (7,7)
6 Orderly way to serve the hard stuff (4)
7 Stylish, soft fabric is stylish (2,5)
8 Manage to live harmoniously (3,2)
9 Good for you, the house is clearly haunted! (5,3,6)
15 He gives the same number to Regina (5)
16 Simpleton leaves a pub in New York (5)
18 Repaired pine desk with just a lovely surface (4-4)
20 In retrospect no single story gave much pleasure (7)

21 One flower shaped like a needle (7)
22 Scratched the ground while Dad tied the knot (5)
25 Fancy man pursues wife (4)
26 Man's house may be entered by them (4)

ACROSS

6 Ambassador, given a port, tips topsy-turvy (4,4,5)
8 Pole held firm – that brings him luck (6)
9 State where soldiers lead the people, perhaps (8)
10 Whoever hid my weeder? (3)
11 Band is second? Rubbish! (6)
12 Ban moral slippage as deviant (8)
14 Pulling up and stretching to see (7)
16 Lines on label showing how to behave when drinking? (3-4)
20 Flew into the Dutch capital to give speech (8)
23 Anti-Philistine boy taking in a literary work (6)
24 Play part in work of government (3)
25 Letter – 0? (8)
26 Elderly in damage from freeze (4,2)
27 Brace oneself to get sand in the mouth? (4,4,5)

DOWN

1 Threat of penalty contains trouble (8)
2 Line of Londoners, from other end of country? (8)
3 Refuge for one beaten by soldiers (7)
4 Make cut in his music? (6)
5 I belong – so give me medal, right? (6)
6 Courage disintegrating? Very sad (5-8)
7 Bull to show fury with European (4,3,6)
13 Sweeper on boat? (3)
15 Popular-sounding pub (3)
17 Horribly tease the artistic type (8)
18 Animal transporter has brawl inside vehicle (8)
19 Lend ear, anyway, to the wise (7)
21 Man I reach is crazy (6)
22 Girl to cut and run (6)

ACROSS

1 Important question of the elder offspring? (5,5)
9 Famous Italian seen back in Florence (4)
10 Fan of sickness benefit? (10)
11 Call for superior judgment (6)
12 Reported to be held at gun-point (7)
15 Old master of the Exchange Rate Mechanism in turn-about (7)
16 Ventured again to take father out (5)
17 He may supply arresting information (4)
18 Play group (4)
19 Submits to a diver's complaint (5)
21 Briefly, I draw no new conclusion (2,1,4)
22 A change in dates offered as an alternative (7)
24 Avoided potential duel with editor (6)
27 Oddly comic place associated with a criminal, perhaps (10)
28 Stuff to study for exam (4)
29 Long leases needed for a place to live in America (3,7)

DOWN

2 Being awkward, mean to get the last word (4)
3 Dull-witted, note, after punishing bouts (6)
4 I will shortly become accustomed to being maltreated (3-4)
5 Place to view, we hear (4)
6 Grenade thrown in temper (7)
7 Check one's speed (10)
8 You may get it in the neck when you detain the boss (6-4)
12 Shared secret belief (10)
13 Informal speech (10)
14 Old-fashioned but popular with the boys (5)
15 Top scorer's off-drive (5)

19 Boring tool commercial interrupts fight (7)
20 Outstanding winter feature (7)
23 A time for high-handedness (6)
25 Experts break the case (4)
26 Name expert seen about skin problem (4)

ACROSS

1 They are bound to belong to the same union (7,3,4)

9 It's to do with the marriage altar I'm decorating (7)

10 Manage reporting wrongdoing first despite having a fainting fit (7)

11 Hurry with big end or crossbar (4)

12 Cheese that's pale, richly mixed (10)

14 Grasp Leonard, head of chapter, in church (6)

15 Awful fuss Bill made despite being perfectly happy (8)

17 Catch one's zip perhaps (8)

18 Fellows more than half agree that it's mad (6)

21 A time, a time in prison in one continuous period (2,1,7)

22 Many a bone found in bed (4)

24 Issued instructions for concise edition (7)

25 Idea produced all the same by model (7)

26 Fire or vote for wealthy consumer (8,6)

DOWN

1 Epic crime perpetrated by Head Office first (7)

2 Jumpy dog? (8-7)

3 Before the stake (4)

4 Old Penny gave everybody a shilling in an American city! (6)

5 Pair blown under the bridge (8)

6 Gain by one city or another (10)

7 The way we read of a Conservative gain (4,4,2,5)

8 Jack Kelly could have the good side (6)

13 Accurate but inartistic presumably (10)

16 One back in the team? (8)

17 Fat alongside hanging loosely (6)

19 Throws three times to get the shellfish (7)

20 One little creature endlessly vinegary (6)

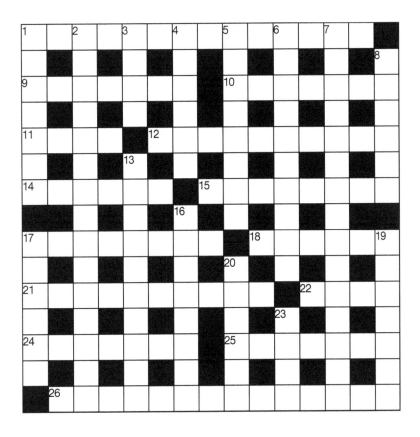

23 It will be a sign for the future when Georgia leaves the wine-shop (4)

9

ACROSS

1 A romance where nothing's right (4-5)
9 Hope is a feature of the church (6)
10 Tiny trace may lead to conviction (9)
11 Decline with little hesitation (6)
12 "To die will be an awfully big —— " (J M Barrie's *Peter Pan*) (9)
13 Gloss over (6)
17 Tot worrying dad (3)
19 Blows up and so shows to advantage (4,3)
20 Notices conveying compliments (7)
21 Some of the gentry are very irritating (3)
23 Singer suffering a breakdown getting leave (6)
27 Offering transport to people is a bloomer! (9)
28 Approached tight newsman (6)
29 Where rail-travellers find the fare (6-3)
30 The guy avoiding a woman turned colour (6)
31 All men do! (4,5)

DOWN

2 Drove madly round to get exhausted (6)
3 The egghead joins up, gaining respect (6)
4 Cheats playing pontoon? (6)
5 Having finished work, went to bed (7)
6 Probing into a variety of pies over a period (9)
7 Terrifying experience of the dark horse (9)
8 Callous fellow, quite plain-speaking (9)
14 Greatness unfortunately makes enemies (9)
15 Check about a writer's hoard (5,4)
16 Hungered possibly, receiving nothing, and got more harsh (9)
17 A very short distance behind (3)
18 Boring prohibitionist (3)
22 Person facing facts about a certain leaning (7)

24 A little fiend in general, that's the conclusion (6)

25 Greek character without a casual shirt? Shame! (6)

26 Advocates entering burning city (6)

ACROSS

1 Barred view, sadly, of house-sparrow? (6,4)
6 Complacent, knocking back sweets (4)
9 Attractive girl liable to change into something more comfortable (10)
10 In the past but never again? (4)
13 Henley's first boat-crews in a position of power (7)
15 Certain in ancient city to find an unscrupulous money-lender (6)
16 Earliest word for throwing money around table-top (6)
17 Scottish blonde noted by Bizet (4,4,2,5)
18 Greek workers providing endowments (6)
20 Where giants walked a National Trust border? (6)
21 As dirty, perhaps, as a butterfly (7)
22 Rear end of queue (4)
25 Four-week period when normal hunt is sabotaged (5,5)
26 Band call (4)
27 Confines joint in office of American doctor (10)

DOWN

1 Extra broad (4)
2 See one as well in alluvial soil (4)
3 One may remove section of opera, serialized (6)
4 Urban dealings by arrangement here, in church fete? (5-3-3,4)
5 Present report (6)
7 Peak of Parisian art? (10)
8 The men grub around for a talented American gardener (5,5)
11 He must always emerge as top-drawer type (10)
12 Brooding male in bankruptcy (10)
13 Solitary people see motorway cutting through county (7)

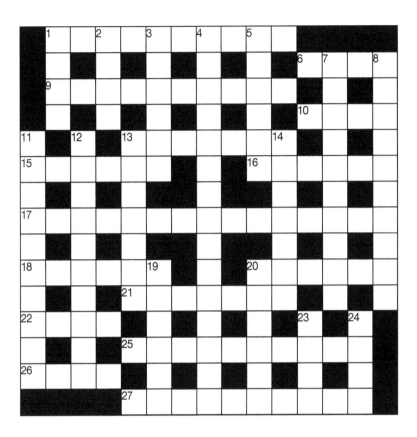

14 What may be picked up by the beak? (7)
19 Planet making a change of course under the sun (6)
20 Pilot in marina out of place (6)
23 Tutankhamen's inner symbol of eternal life (4)
24 Store to give away (4)

11

ACROSS

6 Accountant unpopular at the library? (10)
8 A word of assent from those who assent (4)
9 Resolve hardens in the Jewish council (9)
11 Leave out returning medic with sex appeal (4)
12 Cotton manufacturer shows spirit (3)
13 Broke engagement when summoned elsewhere (6,3)
16 General manager confronts an FBI agent (1-3)
17 Minute portions for dessert? (7)
18 Asked home by Violet and Edward (7)
20 A burden on America (4)
21 A name best used to denote degradation (9)
23 Female hothead about to suffer a reversal (3)
24 Some powerful narcotics for a badly broken bone (4)
25 Stevedores work there at the bar (2,3,4)
29 A cap on the summit (4)
30 Work as a fireman? Get away! (2,2,6)

DOWN

1 Lots of money spent on gambling (4)
2 Hide a second family (4)
3 Old Iranian from the Eastern Mediterranean initially (4)
4 Cock-fight dispute made him murder Cock Robin (7)
5 Male with dementia made to take many a drug (10)
7 Call on burglar's accomplice for reserve funds (4-5)
8 Not short of a first team close by (9)
10 Henry is hard on a trainee (3)
13 Chars at night to gain freedom from debt (5,5)
14 Make haste to appear quick-witted (4,5)

15 In the final act an auditor is winning (9)
19 Some Italian requires a suite (7)
22 Upsetting mother is senseless (3)
26 German banker emerges from hotel bedroom (4)
27 Set it in a ring, old chum! (4)
28 Lean over to pull up a vegetable (4)

ACROSS

1 Have a wonderful time as mountaineer? (3,3,4,5)
9 Partisan, but unreliable (9)
10 Some awful tract from an extremist (5)
11 What it costs to send Gestapo wild (7)
12 Broadcast chief is a fool (7)
13 Child thus given name (3)
14 Catching distance? (7)
17 What's viciously said in row gets contempt (7)
19 No member of old family gets out of bed with a jump (7)
22 Points to Mediterranean island to hide (7)
24 Frequently take money from attic (3)
25 It's standard to cut vegetable (7)
26 Take salt with a single shellfish (7)
28 Presses chains (5)
29 Carlton to broadcast singer (9)
30 Shopworkers' time off – a midwinter afternoon? (5,7,3)

DOWN

1 Not apparent one's next in line (4,11)
2 One agrees to come to these school periods (5)
3 Pig clean? Nonsense! (7)
4 Very saintly, but have position in army (7)
5 Judy's wreath? (7)
6 Son with lots of pages as escorts (7)
7 Keen for advancement, but taken home sick (2,3,4)
8 Donne, my ancestor, used oddly to be very formal (5,2,8)
15 River rose in spate – filling this? (9)
16 Time to speak out for us (3)
18 Carp served in cider (3)

20 Pardon for little woman keeping home (7)
21 Current dilapidated state of coalpit (7)
22 Adds colour, say, to Surrey town (7)
23 Companion has a smile of ruefulness (7)
27 Made to run smoothly, though a little drunk (5)

ACROSS

1 Court verdict on Eve? (5,8)
10 Unnecessary loss of a point irritates (7)
11 Sustain in hours of trouble (7)
12 Those who lose control in rows may catch it (4)
13 Gets the one-fifty in time, being nimble (5)
14 It may be well-worn and well-used (4)
17 A part that can't be matched (7)
18 Bearing out what one would be rude to do (5,2)
19 In piping form (7)
22 Pride in its arrival is no sin for the parents (4-3)
24 Tree father found in America (4)
25 MP and Sue frolic in the foam (5)
26 Recommended course for Parliament (4)
29 A water-bed? (7)
30 So-called lion man abroad (7)
31 Condensed tune, possibly piped (10,3)

DOWN

2 Country music composer (7)
3 I must leave firm, betrayed (4)
4 Love things to be settled right away (2,5)
5 Cool beat from the backing group (3,4)
6 Mind how we appear in Paris (4)
7 Mince pie and preserve for a gourmet (7)
8 The drink to lay one low? (5-3,5)
9 Glass-cutter? (4,2,1,6)
15 A sweet sort of baby (5)
16 Newly-wed given key to chamber? (5)
20 Boasting about a number well done (7)
21 About to be given beans? Push off (7)
22 Expresses sorrow when the last men are out (7)
23 Put a chit in for wine (7)
27 Click! And it's a photograph! (4)
28 Between-maid perhaps (4)

ACROSS

1 Man accompanying a European queen (7)
5 Thoroughly getting to the bottom of it? (2,5)
9 Agreement doctor can arrange (9)
10 Jack turned to Sarah at the lowest level (5)
11 Leapt over the crease (5)
12 Point of attack (9)
13 Sailor man wearing waterproof (9)
16 Savoury for good man in the river (5)
17 The graduate first to take the plunge (5)
18 Bent opening in a wall? (3-6)
20 Go round a heap of snow to find the spray (9)
23 In Limoges, sold plaster of Paris (5)
25 Virginia in row on the sofa (5)
26 Type of car working by itself! (9)
27 Said knight's title? (7)
28 Where grass is dried in the upper room? (7)

DOWN

1 Sailor has shot at Kitty (7)
2 Knight lost a lot of the weapon (5)
3 Reversal of direction concerning refurbished cafe (5-4)
4 The high spots of a South American tour (5)
5 No, we think it's wrong to be initiated (2,3,4)
6 Exclude from French room in a public house (5)
7 Had been under some irresistible influence (9)
8 Leave one in the storage area a year (7)
14 Fetching dog (9)
15 A way to avoid friction (9)
16 Narrow sticky item one has forgotten the name of (9)
17 Sidney taken in by the workers as well (7)
19 Lumber over damaged engraved design (7)
21 Girl – and no mistake (5)

22 Model with restless desire is not a very big person (5)

24 Receiver to begin working (3,2)

15

ACROSS

1 Hides pains following cold (6)
4 Sneer at a composer of music (8)
9 A club well-qualified persons run (6)
10 On-and-off restriction of water-usage (8)
12 There's need for a break in the garden (4)
13 Support a number, as is permissible (5)
14 The monarch in a foreign, poetic land (4)
17 One whose practice it is to manipulate others (12)
20 Upper-class students (5-7)
23 Some people appear allergic to such fruit (4)
24 Weary of it all, but got through (5)
25 Mail distribution in the capital (4)
28 Gather to look at the roadside (8)
29 The Italian, a writer, backing an Asian (6)
30 Separate the underworld on a Mediterranean island (8)
31 Home alternative for the shrewd man (6)

DOWN

1 Force to include an award for relations (8)
2 Superficial means of improving the image (8)
3 Discharge when time's up (4)
5 Transport charges? (8,4)
6 See some ladies' pyjamas (4)
7 A 16 prepared for flotation (6)
8 Making a request in the manner of royalty (6)
11 A bit of chicken and a festive trifle? (12)
15 Being old, is quite possibly hard (5)
16 The management body to get onto (5)
18 It's doubtful the male worker will accept rest (8)
19 For sale: ripe produce grown by a nurseryman (8)
21 A quarter stepped out at intervals (6)

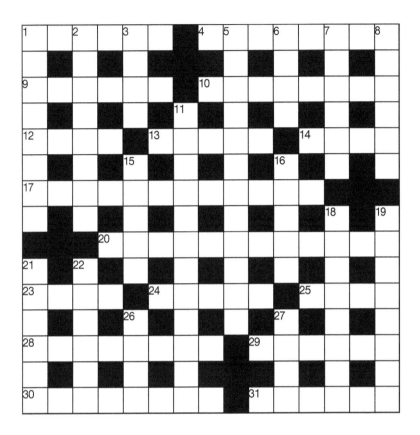

22 Brags about few family members (6)

26 A noble look (4)

27 Only a part of some recent investigations (4)

ACROSS

  1 Girl with a name in new fresco, nothing less (7)
  5 Tendency to be crooked (4)
  9 Carelessly, can miss so called deliveries (6-5,4)
10 Mid-off takes field in unpleasant jumper (4)
11 Edge of motorway illuminated all round (5)
12 Wife to strike for a shoulder-stole? (4)
15 Lower or lengthen dress (3,4)
16 Stern champion showing wry face (7)
17 Tangle we eased out? (7)
19 Hounds in British estate (7)
21 Bottle of Greek and Italian vermouth (4)
22 Loud stringed instrument that is played in the wind (5)
23 Sated in dreadful luncheon (4)
26 Accomplished event, going too far in darkroom (15)
27 River erosion (4)
28 Shoots for greens? (7)

DOWN

  1 Maximum holding of western dollars? (7)
  2 American intern treated this old hearty (7,7)
  3 Traffic-marker once damaged (4)
  4 Notices torn up in passage (7)
  5 Attitude of relation? (7)
  6 Smell of one's cooking (4)
  7 Cuts in energy twice bring blackout (7)
  8 Agency of Foreign Office supporting alliance (8,6)
13 Boudoir of a cellist, say? (5)
14 Original tree on street (5)
17 How to address Italian chap in foreign regions (7)
18 Knocked up for rescue (7)
19 Tablets dished out in Bosworth and Hastings, possibly (7)

20 Presents arms with an instrument on board (7)
24 Advantage of the bearded, generally? (4)
25 Spring's incentive, fame (4)

ACROSS

1 Leading the way with a flame-thrower (7,3,5)
9 So learn about the city saved by Joan of Arc (7)
10 Keeping records is the feller's job (7)
11 Swoop made on a drinking-den (4)
12 Copper catches lad pocketing two bottle-openers (5)
13 A handsome French murder victim (4)
16 Lancastrian foe it's risky to upset (7)
17 Sine qua non for a high-flyer (7)
18 Drop in for a little Yorkshire pudding (7)
21 The railway should have arranged transport (7)
23 Just open to serve a glass of ale (4)
24 Godly man needs a quiet hide-away (5)
25 A shade risqué (4)
28 One so unpunctual must be set apart (7)
29 Old Tom initially included in this French group (7)
30 Producing heavy machinery requires power supply (10,5)

DOWN

1 Generally having a pronounced accent (7,8)
2 Typically shown by the retiring Italian fan (3,4)
3 Single mother who leads the faithful in prayer (4)
4 Travel to athletics events in Hampshire (7)
5 Henry and I save fish (7)
6 Vulgar habits son acquired on return (4)
7 Good-humoured query by intellectual self-doubter (7)
8 Allowed colony to find lawful end to dispute (5,10)
14 In two days I eventually solved the riddle (5)
15 Sound way to get a country house (5)
19 Tactical unit also involved in the scheme (7)
20 Withdraw to negotiate new terms (7)

21 Instrument needed by singer in performance (7)
22 Lady enlivened by festive meal (7)
26 Fine bazaar (4)
27 Remain staunch (4)

ACROSS

1 *Hamlet* is tricky to understand? How you tease (4,4,2,3)
7 To be corpulent, boy, is disastrous (5)
8 A piece in ivory made for emperor (9)
9 Effective as policeman? (2,5)
10 Henry greatly irritates the supporters (7)
11 Channel close to point in field (5)
12 Bystander has magazine (9)
14 Reverse support, and plead for a break (4-5)
17 Spot to hold return exercise – military store (5)
19 Worried by this system in the body? (7)
21 Cooked rice is to rot, sadly (7)
22 A lot of money may go on this pet (9)
23 On balance, extremely serious eating leads to being this (5)
24 Kind offer to read the new order (6-7)

DOWN

1 Contemptible, but arousing sympathy (7)
2 Sensitive condition makes everyone turn grey (7)
3 Managed to get central heating for farm (5)
4 Hairpiece looks best on granny (7)
5 Coat, say, chap put arm in (7)
6 Certain, in special delight, to go around to find hidden wealth (8,5)
7 Free haircut as worker's perk? (6,7)
8 Lucky to be not so long in bed (7)
13 Blow up general in explosion (7)
15 Vehicle, a further vehicle, and trailer (7)
16 Poke stick into purple vegetables (7)
17 Indulge girl, a good loser (7)
18 The buildings round here are some of mine (7)
20 Susie's first desire is to be fashionable (5)

ACROSS

1 Relation found in a semi-religious order? (4-7)

9 Haricot bean, for example, not for a starter (3-6)

10 Form of penicillin? (5)

11 Replacing last of the footlights (6)

12 It passes for accommodation by the club (4-4)

13 Released – or shot (3,3)

15 Test food in court (8)

18 Sheridan's captain bales out when in trouble (8)

19 Put off one's retirement (4,2)

21 Cosmetic combination of sauce and jam? (8)

23 Early rail or space traveller (6)

26 All the composer required (5)

27 Newly-formed orchestra has great drawing capacity (9)

28 In organised events rifle club's best side is seen (5,6)

DOWN

1 A troublesome quantity though not beyond your grasp (7)

2 Slow movement produced no advance (5)

3 Liberal peeress (9)

4 The sound of a pig in agreeable surroundings (4)

5 Colourful display of arms (8)

6 Relax the terms of reference (5)

7 A number making a noise in an examination (7)

8 Prevalence of money (8)

14 Arrests drunkard in lift – or drunkards (8)

16 Promise that makes both alter (9)

17 Good man rebuilt a crock – for racing? (5,3)

18 Heavens, what a cast! (3-4)

20 Be nice to a dog and a bird, for example (7)

22 What he does is appropriate (5)

24 Mixed drink five love to imbibe in Russian city (5)
25 It's wrong to raise the pace (4)

ACROSS

1 Company in Greek capital going round under an assumed name (5)

4 They give high-jumpers openings (8)

8 Then part yourself from a gathering of woman only (3-5)

9 Authorise a penalty (8)

11 Jack included bumpy ride later (7)

13 Making things more equal before night begins? (7,2)

15 How goes the enemy? Apparently there's no need to hurry (4,2,2,3,4)

18 Got back ground in a rush (9)

21 Incomplete fragment Penny points out (7)

22 Desiring to remove area with the best seats (8)

24 From *La Scala*, Brian went to an area of south-west Italy (8)

25 Half hope no girl can be found in island capital (8)

26 Shade all over the place – it's very hot here (5)

DOWN

1 How one might be facing punishment whilst bathing? (2,3,5)

2 Middleman's politics? (8)

3 Pleased I had oil removed from the flowers (8)

4 In the foyer, hysterical Welshman (4)

5 Pretentious Greek character doubled up (6)

6 Free gin distribution whilst on horseback (6)

7 Is on another hill in Jerusalem (4)

10 What could be said and done about removing these in an operation perhaps (8)

12 Better shape in the plant (8)

14 A bad state to come to via attractive route through the mountains (6,4)

16 Censure golfer perhaps getting within reach (8)
17 Spider in web directed by divine influence (8)
19 Is able to negotiate first part of Switzerland (6)
20 Seaman to sail, say, down a rockface! (6)
22 Ill-considered outbreak (4)
23 London district had short run for fawn (4)

ACROSS

1 Close a valve thus, perhaps (4,3)
5 Meals for father in breaks from work (7)
9 Play Ted reviewed with expertise (7)
10 Cheerful boy and aunt played together (7)
11 Most inexpensive hat priced wrongly (4,5)
12 Strange how mill-race ends in the lake (5)
13 Hard-hearted king whose widow was merry (5)
15 Move to the middle and compromise (7-3)
17 Reptile giving a girl a lot of trouble (9)
19 Italian capital has nothing for Juliet's husband (5)
22 Have a duty, even if it might be tough? (5)
23 Such a discussion gives opportunity for falling out (4-5)
25 Girl holds bat incorrectly in game (7)
26 Studio that is later converted (7)
27 Arab leaders trembling in speech (7)
28 Arrested missing Pole perhaps, recovered tyre (7)

DOWN

1 Con man turns up in disgrace (7)
2 Discover a foreign planet (7)
3 Scotch governor? (5)
4 Boxer of cunning and power (9)
5 To do so the wrong way will go against the grain (3,2)
6 A driver going round in circles (9)
7 A couple of scraps for bird (7)
8 Yet it's a misplaced feeling of gratification (7)
14 He's not left with support in defence (5,4)
16 Upholstery material that is harsh or rough (9)
17 Not a sum that's incorrect – sums (7)
18 He took in, in wild glee, what was left (7)
20 She makes personal deliveries (7)

21 Arranged, but not voluntary (7)
23 Shows fond regard for the opposite sex (5)
24 Build straight up (5)

ACROSS

1 Striker – but not when he's out (7)
5 How wheels manage detours? (2,5)
9 London circus crossing river first (9)
10 From Ben Nevis, takes the view (5)
11 Port found in the cellar? Never (5)
12 Looking about (9)
13 Hot preacher (9)
16 Reached shirt caught in butter! (3,2)
17 We object to bad smell first from decayed mould (5)
18 Direction minor takes before second half of July capriciously (9)
20 Mongrel angry with food was reported (9)
23 Deceive about fifty – or twice as many (5)
25 It is not true, pair are said to come to a standstill (3,2)
26 Put off most of the trip Dad arranged outside (9)
27 Go back and make another copy (7)
28 Made an indentation but not with companion Edward (7)

DOWN

1 Support record build-up (7)
2 Not such a wild circus performer (5)
3 She takes life seriously (9)
4 Lowest point dinar could reach? (5)
5 Two boys with capital cover in the Highlands (9)
6 Stray dog? (5)
7 Lavish nude performing task within (9)
8 Drink on board (7)
14 Lemons not shaken are likely to drop off! (9)
15 Let down with a set of small type (5-4)
16 Grandmother shortly to discourage another relative (5-4)

17 Someone who does not believe in free speech (7)
19 Bore resigned (7)
21 A most remarkable opening (5)
22 Joanna found in the row in French city (5)
24 Steal a small amount of salt (5)

ACROSS

1 Delivery charge for a flowering plant? (10)
9 A small group, or it could be (4)
10 Having the power to contract for temporary accommodation without phone (10)
11 A hearing device Edward's got (6)
12 Drivers attracting attention in London? (7)
15 Daring to vex a social worker (7)
16 Colourful but unsophisticated (5)
17 Accustomed to being in employment (4)
18 Exceptionally neat mount (4)
19 A drink that's really way-out! (5)
21 Awfully posh Italian opening church refuge (7)
22 Town getting a point over about the air (7)
24 Grace is in love with a liar (6)
27 Time to give encouragement in a mundane way (10)
28 The man turning the French on (4)
29 Even Athens can be divine! (6-4)

DOWN

2 Inspect and put back casual shirt (4)
3 Seeing a painter on holiday is most uncommon (6)
4 Decline to join evil top man (7)
5 Article for which one paid up (4)
6 More behind an old palace (7)
7 Dealt with TT races and scrambles (10)
8 It's OK to tax commercial transport (5-5)
12 Criterion for a Shakespearean role (10)
13 Makes too much of the American president's position (10)
14 Bars put right in the entrance (5)
15 Antelopes, including the little Oriental kind (5)
19 A slight wound that's no handicap (7)

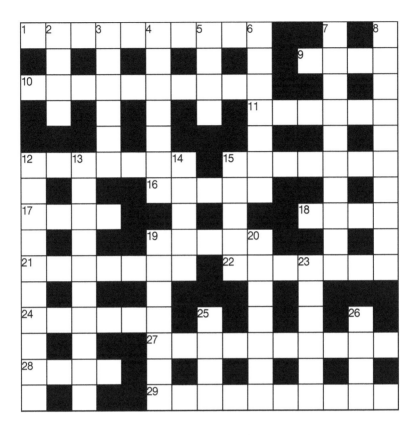

20 The couple most woe-afflicted (7)
23 Turned up issue about irate gypsies (6)
25 Some of them may embrace a girl (4)
26 Large family – many will get canned! (4)

ACROSS

1 Material in carol needs a bit of learning (10)
6 Put up with a nuisance (4)
9 Not yet? Dead right (5)
10 Miss Italy? (9)
12 Getting those that are cast to speak in every possible way (6-7)
14 Type of music boat race crew would like? (3,5)
15 Type of music to make an alto struggle? (6)
17 Nefariously inspecting the cladding (6)
19 Slips and other underwear (8)
21 The two censors in error? Goodness me! (5,3,5)
24 At sea, for the most part (2,3,4)
25 A very expensive bar (5)
26 Fat boy crosses river (4)
27 His notice may appear in newspaper column (10)

DOWN

1 Get money for some counselling (4)
2 It helps one look you in the eye, when giving you the news (7)
3 Try undeniable criminal, but condone offence (4,1,5,3)
4 Gave up work, accepting the inevitable (8)
5 Nigel finally moves to other side of river (5)
7 Nothing to confine thought (7)
8 Mark, say, is leaving set confused (10)
11 May he seek a hobby? He has one already (13)
13 Motionless, like farm animals? (5-5)
16 Spanish town where girl receives amazing tan (8)
18 Hired killer or what he uses (7)
20 Flags, sensing sickness (7)
22 Store oxygen in solid form (5)
23 Cause trouble in prison (4)

ACROSS

1 Inflexibility superior feature of a true Englishman? (5,5,3)

10 Sort out the middle of a tune with the composer (7)

11 Uniform – and it's wearer? (7)

12 Escape from contaminated lake (4)

13 Believes they're used for cargo (5)

14 Female lost her head in Arabia (4)

17 Sympathise with a number drawing unemployment benefit (7)

18 Vexed expression, the pet has died (7)

19 A newspaper giving it a bold presentation (7)

22 Like news maybe, from the Capitol? (7)

24 Detain in a safe place (4)

25 Thrash about the ring showing little craft (5)

26 Organisation usually accepting responsibility (4)

29 We're yet in the process of growing (3-4)

30 Road not affected by the storm (7)

31 View of one who should know better (6,7)

DOWN

2 About to be put up in school ground (7)

3 Number four iron taken out (4)

4 Liberate one soul in torment (7)

5 Notice cut out and displayed (7)

6 The right time for fashion (4)

7 Up in the air amid the dance (2,5)

8 Spare lockers? (9,4)

9 Pretty conventional symbol of Unions (6-7)

15 Drive from tee in open country (5)

16 Open a fresh page (5)

20 Workers spread wood polish (4-3)

21 The talk of the district (7)

	1	2		3		4		5		6		7		
8														9
10							11							
12				13					14					
			15					16						
17						18								
19	20			21		22			23					
24			25					26						
		27				28								
29						30								
	31													

22 We stop dancing after a sort of square dance (3-4)

23 Once VAT has been sorted out, obtain old Portuguese coin (7)

27 Not working for nothing (4)

28 It flies about in different directions (4)

26

ACROSS

1 He's in order, saying nothing (8)
9 Something that started once upon a time presumably (3,5)
10 Many an involuntary sound that is elegant! (4)
11 Corn to be a problem in the future? (7,5)
13 Passage of power (8)
15 Lady having the same fish (6)
16 In the team a hospital nurse (4)
17 Indian price coming from Mainz... (5)
18 ...reportedly look for another Indian (4)
20 Count on husband entering force (6)
21 Keeps oneself from doing something in the choruses (8)
23 Not out of hand when governed from above (5,7)
26 Four to one, a Russian (4)
27 Sea of floating vegetation? (8)
28 Mark and I log out remarkable weight (8)

DOWN

2 It could hold a lot of champagne for the old king (8)
3 Art gallery? (7-5)
4 Incursion, having a rod in pickle? (6)
5 Grave of a cat, second class (4)
6 Madden new order of the French entering supplementary material (8)
7 Bird's double act (4)
8 Canine with one or two features? (3-5)
12 Anticipating store falling over (12)
14 Elevator said to be used in the bathroom (5)
16 A platitude about leading lady's unselfish concern for others (8)
17 Mark on suit containing money (8)

19 Family has revolutionised it in Zaire (8)

22 Replacing French complaint with due ceremony (6)

24 It is dismal being kept in it (4)

25 Corner disallowed presumably (4)

ACROSS

7 Consequence of second Shaw play presented (8)
9 Time to retire for leaderless leader-writer (6)
10 Port – a place of safety (4)
11 Means to secure some artist's work (7,3)
12 Showing nous in coming agreement (6)
14 Barter, being out of ready money (8)
15 Offensive rows within the Church (6)
17 Shrewd man offering home to simple soldiers (6)
20 Breed of pigs for country folk? (8)
22 Scares off a display of affection (6)
23 4 wants help with tax (6-4)
24 Unable to speak in a wheedling way (4)
25 Meal prepared by one-time coppers inside (6)
26 Just a hymn or a full service? (8)

DOWN

1 New variety of corn – said to be bitter (8)
2 Related in painstaking fashion (4)
3 A quarter pull up and park (6)
4 23 has come with dire problem (8)
5 Person telephoning to accept post as compère (10)
6 Take care of valuable china for the future (6)
8 Doctor the woman imbibing drink (6)
13 Cope with direction and angle (10)
16 Regulation colours (8)
18 Ringing to storm about Oriental issue (8)
19 About fifty scoffed but set forth (6)
21 Girl with a liver disorder (6)
22 Hands over the Spanish embroidery (6)

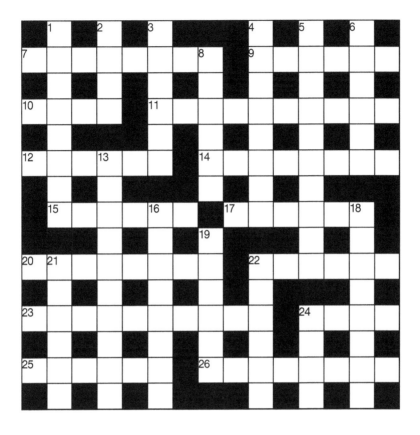

24 A club, that's the firm's aspiration! (4)

ACROSS

1 A kiss in love story said to make a neat ending (6)
4 Light equipment for miner and motorist (8)
9 Unveil the ultimate sex-op surgery (6)
10 Bar on a flight (5-3)
12 Spoil the sound of an instrument (4)
13 A flower possibly open before the end of July (5)
14 A state of pure chaos (4)
17 Performed with a high degree of skill (12)
20 Not good value for a bun, unfortunately (12)
23 Get money for working in near chaos (4)
24 Dishonest, and wary about publicity (5)
25 Pool giving pleasure to many (4)
28 Vehicle needs protection for the front (8)
29 English country property (6)
30 Caledonian will be put out by this cost (8)
31 Quiet place for a school break (6)

DOWN

1 Charge too much? (8)
2 To surpass score is excellent (3-5)
3 In a way, it means this month (4)
5 Won't want to, particularly if remarks are in bad taste! (3,4,5)
6 Spot the wimp (4)
7 Following inflation it offers comfort to the holiday-maker (3-3)
8 Party leader's contempt for the platform (6)
11 Hears pianola transcription for wind instruments (7,5)
15 Improve on a repair (5)
16 Cattle, it's said, may be gathered (5)
18 A doubter disposed to be stubborn (8)
19 Not paying attention in Leeds, she crashed (8)
21 Number of mischievous characters in digs (6)

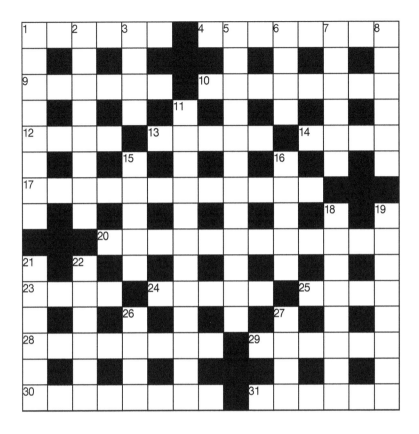

22 Rob irregular corporal of horse (6)
26 Barely deserved (4)
27 Land that lies around in the water? (4)

29

ACROSS

1 A person in the know will get the contents right (7)
5 Sets about girls (7)
9 A pressing time? (7)
10 No longer simple to account for (7)
11 Like transcribing a priest's letters (9)
12 Sound fish from which to breed (5)
13 A blunder some terrorists commit (5)
15 Where youngsters alone are nurtured (9)
17 Those taps fixed very quickly (9)
19 Bond readily returned a key taken (5)
22 Plants for a dry situation free from pollution (5)
23 Using a brush in totally dotty fashion (9)
25 Hard extremity breaks one in the end (3-4)
26 Take the air and cheer up! (7)
27 House rule (7)
28 Reading building with a textured surface (7)

DOWN

1 Repeat it over a long period, note (7)
2 Caresses taken the wrong way by a dancer (7)
3 The German going round American centre gets a towel (5)
4 Virtuous rogue. This must be erroneous! (9)
5 Flies many members (5)
6 Refer to a page with audacious article in (9)
7 The way a talking bird shows resilience (7)
8 Faithful as serving men (7)
14 Robs a home – maybe finds large quantities of drink (9)
16 Quietly staying in control of things (9)
17 Place in a vegetable container, as laid down (7)
18 Swelling number backing up a medical specialist (7)
20 Work in one – forward thinking (7)

21 Intellectual press chief (7)
23 Woman in a rush? (5)
24 All over a cereal food (5)

30

ACROSS

1 In Derby sweepstake, one might hope to succeed unfairly (4,1,4,3)
8 Splendid – a Georgian town (7)
9 Such pompous speech, given artificial elevation? (7)
11 Doctor takes anything that's beer (7)
12 Sort of bar not offering generous measures (7)
13 Flow control very necessary in valley (5)
14 Pure as the flowing river (9)
16 Soldiers in front of tower showing muscle (9)
19 Plot the French growth in Canada (5)
21 Beg spirit to bring wisdom (7)
23 Fruit is an essential – a second brought back (7)
24 Crossing both poles in characteristic garb (7)
25 Farming only while young? (7)
26 On which skater's performance should be proportionally marked? (7,5)

DOWN

1 Not a straight-line queue? (7)
2 Bend in the road that's forked in Italy (7)
3 Lodging suitable to house people after rat's got out (9)
4 Almost rate as partners for Jenny (5)
5 Item for painter – there's more spare (7)
6 Not allowed to hide point in brief communication (7)
7 Betray with handwriting how one made lots of money (4,4,4)
10 Zone visited by accident needing official aid (8,4)
15 As parties go wild, they need indulgent hosts (9)
17 One high up on board sees a pilot's error (7)
18 Woken to find river running through a road (7)

19 Carpet laid out for old empress (7)
20 Robin's coat (7)
22 Not all meat enjoyably consumed (5)

31

ACROSS

6 Suiting the seasons? (6,3,4)
8 Depression after an attack, perhaps (6)
9 False story about ringleader produces bad feeling (8)
10 Priest quite absorbed in his religion (3)
11 Reinforce complaint that's raised (4,2)
12 See great changes in economy travel (8)
14 Lavish praise (7)
16 Learned English with Trudie, perhaps (7)
20 Possible secret of not having to pay (4,4)
23 They're paid for it on board after six (6)
24 About to swallow duck eggs (3)
25 Being so one may react rashly with unusual ill-grace (8)
26 Take things the wrong way (6)
27 Its staff run a meals-on-wheels service (10,3)

DOWN

1 Files put in the wrong order with malicious intent (8)
2 Pet cried out, on its last legs (8)
3 From a service angle is careless in dress (7)
4 Publicity in place of helpful suggestions (6)
5 Top car manufacturer who takes prize (6)
6 Style of architecture that may be dropped (13)
7 Considered the matter closed? (7,2,4)
13 Some of the musicians get the bird (3)
15 He gets red if a stranger addresses him (3)
17 Hot-rod driving is completely absorbing (8)
18 Separate – that's abundantly clear (8)
19 Planet rising in temperature (7)
21 This religious belief is held by our opponents (6)
22 When students may collect on the streets (3-3)

32

ACROSS

1 Unseemly support in the mire swirling (8)
6 Impish person priest converted (6)
9 Grub found by Girl Guide leaders in collapsed moat (6)
10 Left at home with nurse coming round (8)
11 Fancy piece of music? (8)
12 The way a student follows? (6)
13 Replaced hot, coarse food on the way (12)
16 Primate has a problem with a tree (6-6)
19 I went round with Penny once, went round (6)
21 Gave a new heading to letter I'd rewritten (8)
23 Tending to be smartening a horse? (8)
24 Extremely clever somewhat in part (6)
25 Animal, if here, must be removed (6)
26 It is boring to dress a number of people (8)

DOWN

2 Scanty, having nothing more than silver inside (6)
3 Correct claim (5)
4 Favoured explanation about one's cat? (3,6)
5 Italian dish is right first, a German concluded (7)
6 The boy in charge of sound (5)
7 What cabinetmaker might do with the pack! (9)
8 Cherish the hoard (8)
13 Mimicking what the stripper is doing (6,3)
14 Dictionary used by newspaper almost at all times (9)
15 In the furze, couple went into decline apparently (3,5)
17 Just standing (7)
18 It's thrown from ships and aircraft in the morning (6)
20 Machine that needs less water? (5)
22 Head lock (5)

33

ACROSS

1 Was red as could be leaving the beach (8)
5 Alarms and anxiety aboard ship (6)
9 The French back new unit-trust that's humanitarian (8)
10 To adulterate alcoholic drink gives an edge (6)
11 Scorn but study allure (8)
12 Markets about a thousand scents (6)
14 A military commander should be quite impervious (10)
18 Taxes a peer may well find cause great irritation (10)
22 Drawing small boat (6)
23 Soldiers authorised hold the front in question (8)
24 The coolness of a quiet trainee with incomplete bomb (6)
25 Facing work, attitudinise about it (8)
26 The conclusion is not all attend in good faith (6)
27 Get at aid organisation, being perturbed (8)

DOWN

1 Inadequate, throwing many into a panic (6)
2 The man's not given a rise in any situation (6)
3 A journalist holding public transport is exploited (6)
4 Withdraws papers said to be controversial (10)
6 Winsome child preparing for a fight (8)
7 One of the guns returned – had a meal to order (8)
8 Repeatedly produce notes needed by a prison (8)
13 A means of securing clean linen (7-3)
15 Convince people coins used are counterfeit (8)
16 Identified the youth pocketing a peach (8)
17 He's above all mundane things (8)
19 Start putting points to a solicitor (3,3)

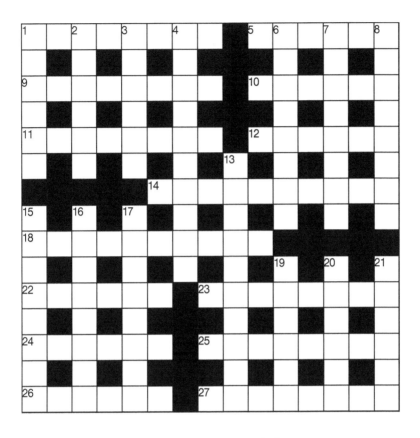

20 A trial could result in the noose! (6)

21 There's a series of races – aim to be there (6)

34

ACROSS

1 Hero-subject due for a change as novel stonemason (4,3,7)

9 Shed, substandard, is abandoned (4-3)

10 Breathe through nose very loudly in Neil's trouble (7)

11 Large building foundation (4)

12 Day interminable with no one to turn to (10)

14 Apply oneself to rigging (6)

15 Explain crack? (8)

17 Cocktails taken in combinations? (8)

18 Celebrity goes to church with such formality (6)

21 Remarkable new name in carbolic acid (10)

22 Work in it back to front as some protection from sun (4)

24 Enthral, in French style, with *Valse Exotique* (7)

25 Oil near out? There's a banking flap! (7)

26 Demurest tenant thrown out for using restraint (14)

DOWN

1 Kitty with fellow taking cannabis (7)

2 Refugee from clan predisposed to scatter (9,6)

3 Excessively long bill, for example? (4)

4 Force used by thief for tampering (6)

5 For example, Bede is represented as overwhelmed with requests (8)

6 Presentation of a tot? (10)

7 Brushing-up studies, say (9,6)

8 Tricky question for Badger – and Ratty, initially (6)

13 Choose to make a speech for all voters (10)

16 Ivy, for example, wearing Sunday shoes (8)

17 Private papers sorted out (6)

19 Means of fixing locks out of the rain (7)

20 California prohibit a changing-hut on the beach? (6)

23 Dismal conservative? (4)

35

ACROSS

1 Man on motorway has scope for part of the planet (10)
6 Come up against an objection (4)
9 May get on as a rule (5)
10 A light covering (9)
12 It's what a ledger records presumably (6,2,5)
14 And not the navy line in London (8)
15 It's nonsense to dispose of his book, nothing less (6)
17 Cretan collected a heavenly drink (6)
19 More rugged rig Grace erected! (8)
21 No lack of room for astronauts (6,2,5)
24 Circular wriggler? (9)
25 Amount to pay for a piano? (5)
26 Daughter ran off with stitch (4)
27 Dot has been abducted, I agree with you (5,5)

DOWN

1 Horse is in some shackles (4)
2 After half-time, I have the right fur (7)
3 Dedicated to celibacy? (6-7)
4 Official stamp on building record (8)
5 Lover gets no addition to capital (5)
7 Cupholder has a party about five – it's a boastful show! (7)
8 Do not worry at that place repeatedly (5,5)
11 Jack to obtain, after resting, an easy victim (7,6)
13 Unimaginative one in Paris drew breath (10)
16 An inexperienced fellow starting university? (8)
18 Peg one who threatens to win at chess so it is said (7)
20 Cold bag that might be drifting in the sea (7)
22 Moulding rings about short book (5)
23 Silent god (4)

36

ACROSS

1 Specially order running water from doorman (14)
9 Have a high old time? (4,2,2)
10 Indian beginning to mow through the weaker batsmen (5)
12 Only give a couple of seconds to good book (4)
13 Fainting at this Sandhurst parade? (7,3)
15 Put by Oriental wine as memento (8)
16 Came in to organise show-house (6)
18 He's frequently called over in the game (6)
20 Put one's foot down, getting out of engagement (8)
23 Aspersions engulf the wrong islander (10)
24 Indicate to write one's name (4)
26 Prone to telling fibs? (5)
27 Dull club used once for evening work (4,4)
28 Offender that's shopped, taken by him? (5,9)

DOWN

2 For a gold piece, I do more work (7)
3 As roads may dangerously be, around December 1st? (4)
4 Checks collection, and puts money on (8)
5 Be against work with model (6)
6 Vital loans taken out by footballers (5,5)
7 Curious staff seen in fictional chambers (7)
8 Vendor that automatically coins it in (4,7)
11 Terrier sailor's given to prime minister (4,7)
14 Tabloid's star columnist (10)
17 About to run away to the point (8)
19 Divine decree introduced by priest briefly (7)
21 Journey to oil-processing port (7)
22 Stabbed king – fined, beaten up (6)
25 Quiz in chemistry includes this element (4)

37

ACROSS

1 Appears wet, perhaps, but may be recycled (5,5)
9 Satisfied with a quarter measure (4)
10 Flycatcher (7,3)
11 Develop and go round topless (6)
12 They hope to find you well (7)
15 Initial word of the companion in the morning (7)
16 A temple ornament (5)
17 Sound vision required by a city developer (4)
18 Turn crazy with shock (4)
19 Brew of beer left to rise (5)
21 They swear they'll try in the box (7)
22 Student deserved to become academic (7)
24 Old saw that's lost its cutting edge (6)
27 Warn omelet is off, but may still be eaten (5-5)
28 Male chorus provides an encore (4)
29 Measures not intended to be taken seriously? (5,5)

DOWN

2 Rising resort includes lake and mountains (4)
3 Cleans up when diet is put out (6)
4 Meaning it's almost unadulterated wine (7)
5 Leave with uncle (4)
6 Novel title of Esau's mother (7)
7 Capital footwear (10)
8 Decided to be resolute (10)
12 A person known for putting on airs? (4,6)
13 Certain to get drunk on Adam's ale (10)
14 Warning! This woman is dangerous (5)
15 A character in *The Tempest* – or one in *Lear* perhaps (5)
19 Restoration novel in authentic setting (7)
20 It was in form when young (7)
23 Venerate an American patriot (6)

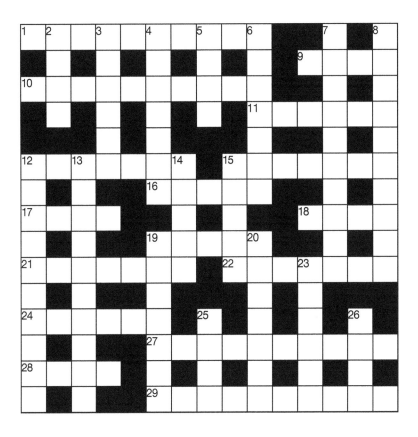

25 Speculator, a good man with silver (4)

26 From the sound of it they are spirited cat-calls! (4)

38

ACROSS

1 Back up during games (7)
5 Stored a crumble that had been baked (7)
9 Endlessly troublesome prickle (5)
10 Field Marshal who provided the stove! (9)
11 Sole supplier (10)
12 Close imitation of a screech-owl (4)
14 In accord with conditions in America (6,6)
18 Separation of oddfellows that are taken in by extra-terrestrial (12)
21 Opposition MPs (4)
22 One way and another I will come to a halt (10)
25 Goat prods struggling mollusc (9)
26 Finally inconclusive book (5)
27 About to suspect the fieldwork (7)
28 One who chooses to be at cross purposes? (7)

DOWN

1 Start with well-dressed person from Kent area (3,3)
2 Voting system will unseat the novelist (6)
3 Ron refashioned a mantle elaborately making it decorative (10)
4 A king surrounded by number that had been captured (5)
5 Right beast to blockade port (9)
6 So extremely hazy and grey (4)
7 Doggedness of X taking a large town (8)
8 Converted room used by small creature (8)
13 The look of one who's broke? (5,5)
15 Difficult situation for a drunk to be in? (5,4)
16 Green tea brewed by youngster (8)
17 Showed the importance of bringing back puds (8)
19 Love, it upset the girl (6)
20 Shutter (6)

23 Gun 'e'd cocked, having given it a prod (5)

24 Bedraggled fur wrapped round a German lady (4)

39

ACROSS

1 Drink cider, as broke (7)
5 Relevant article for personnel officers (7)
9 Ham on the turn (7)
10 The party about to return by water (7)
11 Assume one is in the mail (5)
12 A qualification men met – and otherwise (9)
13 Individual with a pragmatic attitude where a catalogue's concerned (7)
14 There's confusion about the trainee's protection (7)
16 Sent a goody-goody inside – so wise (7)
19 Resolve to take some exercise (4,3)
22 The drill-sergeant's revolutionary order (5,4)
24 Being enthusiastic, the Spanish are building (5)
25 Taken in hand by the main supervisor (7)
26 Beat the top man in the rush (7)
27 He sets all straight – it's not left to the queen (7)
28 Appear morose about fine project (4,3)

DOWN

1 Plug sport and PE perhaps (7)
2 Speed back East with a marine (4-3)
3 List canoe usage at the seaside (9)
4 Withdraw troops over a wide area (7)
5 Old soldiers well-used to pulling strings! (7)
6 Stormed at for getting into debt (5)
7 The left capturing a number would be a forewarning (7)
8 Wrestle possibly to perspire profusely (7)
15 Cultivation? (9)
16 Point out to a mad character causing split (7)
17 Questioning the little page getting dressed up (7)
18 One believes the way lies in more sound (7)
19 Finally deals with cranks (5,2)

20 Rings about train crash in Canada (7)
21 Everything in a trial that's most incredible (7)
23 Pay for leading two of trumps and scoff (5)

40

ACROSS

1 Hanger-on given a piastre possibly (8)
5 Being firm over voucher (6)
9 Newsman dealing with alcoholic drink (8)
10 A communal home may well be littered! (6)
12 Names a mutinous sailor (6)
13 Such low prices don't allow of profits (8)
15 Tract of grassland left wild (7)
16 A tale constantly re-read absorbs him (4)
20 Run cut by a quarter (4)
21 Force back transport for fun (7)
25 Batting position for example (8)
26 Where to go to shoot duck? (6)
28 Meals the queen finds a problem (6)
29 Driving one round the bend! (8)
30 Old bailiffs maybe severe (6)
31 Conflict about an inexperienced motorist's window (8)

DOWN

1 "Where there is no vision, the people —— " (*Proverbs, The Old Testament*) (6)
2 The traveller remained for another game (6)
3 Moved quickly, not being suited (8)
4 A joiner making a row (4)
6 Colourful name of a royal house (6)
7 Parcel it out, though there's only a bit (8)
8 Black medick is unique (8)
11 Thanks to exercise the Communist got slimmer (7)
14 A shady character's wounded feelings (7)
17 An enclosed place might be costlier (8)
18 The renegade offered a job scoffed (8)
19 Strange Arab lore concerning trees (8)
22 Run with a note to get something floral (6)

23 Pop round, cutting things fine (6)
24 Small number should overlap or none whatsoever (6)
27 A little sweet-natured mount (4)

41

ACROSS

1 Reactionary clique needed to pave the way (4,4)
5 An unemployed film star is given compensation (6)
9 His headgear leaves collier without injury (8)
10 MP in Communist capital (6)
12 Tend to leap without initial caution? (4,5)
13 Old poet gets house by the sea in France (5)
14 Unsightly mark on a small motor (4)
16 Runs into eccentric parson holding Scottish purse (7)
19 Criticise animal shelter for accommodating motorists (3,4)
21 It keeps the pot nice and warm (4)
24 Affected speech proves minor set-back to trainee (5)
25 Yours truly is the boss (6,3)
27 About to get a ring (6)
28 Everything considered and tired of everything (3,2,3)
29 Sober man in penury is trapped (6)
30 Noted cricketer represented no threat (8)

DOWN

1 I am upset during self-righteous sermon (6)
2 Come quickly to get a stomach flattener! (4-2)
3 Feature on a country in Asia (5)
4 Tenant carries key to get back in (2-5)
6 Meat casseroles suggest luxury living (9)
7 My acer – so unusual a tree (8)
8 Coming down pointedly to record Wagnerian operas (8)
11 In warfare soldiers once appealed to him (4)
15 Dare to hide two-pound note among coins (9)
17 A Channel Island's sewer is environmentally unfriendly (4,4)

18 Escape – for a brief holiday in the sun? (5,3)
20 Family confronts deputy-head in class (4)
21 Arrived by luck at Arthur's court (7)
22 Work in section producing modern pictures (3,3)
23 Collapsed after having got into line (4,2)
26 Choice type (5)

42

ACROSS

1 Where we have our mortgage, free? (2,3,5)
9 Sculpture is ruined (4)
10 Don't take afternoon plane – it's unreliable (3-2-5)
11 Teacher beginning to transform poor batsman (6)
12 Aware monarch wants to receive present (7)
15 One making paper for a poster, perhaps (7)
16 General admission (5)
17 Furnishings of a room may include this (4)
18 Concede victory in Europe to an American soldier (4)
19 Bachelor with one child – what an animal (5)
21 Wet stone – I'm slipping (7)
22 Intelligence – hers is decaying (7)
24 Ring the curator (6)
27 Sort of salesman likely to put his foot in it? (4-2-4)
28 Saddle stitch? (4)
29 Sign on here? (6,4)

DOWN

2 River's wiggly line (4)
3 Tongue man had with tea, say (6)
4 Sentence is suspended (7)
5 Recommend not to start clear-out (4)
6 Commit ten faults – consequence of idleness (7)
7 Burmese hid, surprisingly, near Grimsby (10)
8 Victoria, the queen's, tradesmen? (10)
12 Musical proposition to Catherine (4,2,4)
13 Not caring for debauchery in wine-merchant's (3-7)
14 Harvest gets one right in profit (5)
15 Provide support, enough for poet to keep daughter (5)
19 Visibly masculine, somewhat ardent in bed (7)

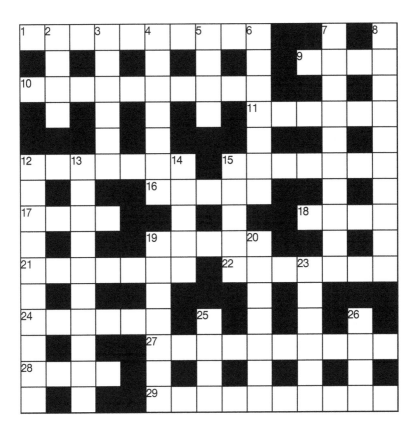

20 Strange thing that's put on late (7)
23 Title announced by composer (6)
25 Youngster left in bed (4)
26 Put on in poor condition (4)

43

ACROSS

6 A non-specialist graduate, I perform autumn jobs (4,2,3,4)

8 A fool it's wrong to help (6)

9 Sort of society in which people want to take part? (8)

10 Expected a letter from a duke (3)

11 Team held by mother to be the tops (6)

12 Honest deal? (8)

14 TV station common to Britain and France (7)

16 He needs a regular supply of drugs to keep going (7)

20 Prank ceased being funny when father came in (8)

23 Soldier dispatched to the lines (6)

24 Current term for a politician (3)

25 Contradictory orders to the yachtsman for more canvas (8)

26 Raid the entrance? (6)

27 The tobacco habit? (7,6)

DOWN

1 Commons vote leads to disagreement (8)

2 One way to check payment by cheque (4-4)

3 Tangled threads are the most difficult (7)

4 A lieutenant bearing one star (6)

5 In this way a West African country becomes East African (6)

6 Mass in its full version (13)

7 Champions away from home? (7,6)

13 A church is one (3)

15 Pan back to a card-game (3)

17 All being well, it should be empty (8)

18 Male bird and plant (8)

19 Resistance to *mal-de-mer*, say, among swimmers (3-4)

21 No way out around the centre, at all events (6)

22 Bill joins a spy organisation, becoming a plant (6)

44

ACROSS

1 Cheerleader backing friends in the fellowship (13)
7 Not a purpose-built structure (5)
8 I put Colin about with pretty formality (9)
9 Do not include Rex in extract (7)
10 Where in America it was fashionable in the past? (7)
11 Some tidy Llandudno beach makes a charming scene (5)
12 Not just having seasonal leaves (9)
14 Shoot some dust-like particles in the explosive mixture (9)
17 Guard low-lying area by church (5)
19 Hundred less cryptic clues I have that are indefinable (7)
21 First gear in the nursery (7)
22 Peruse article about making one's way through the crowd (9)
23 Religious man followed Newton in West Country town (5)
24 Fight after a race? It's a continuous argument (7,6)

DOWN

1 Shy about defeat whilst suffering inner pain (7)
2 Spring examination of the chief citizen (7)
3 Greek style I love that's almost pleasant (5)
4 Love from night on bender (7)
5 Scottish physiologist Daniel in healthy surroundings (7)
6 Official statement made by me possibly with Bond (13)
7 What one hopes to be doing when the numbness has gone (7,6)

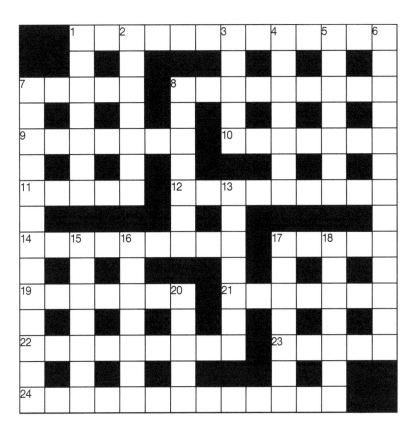

8 I take the stuffing out at the top of the mine-shaft (7)

13 But it does not stop the listener from receiving a radio communication (7)

15 Uncharged particle, turn one out (7)

16 Japanese art increasing, say (7)

17 Stately flight to go swiftly on the way with father inside (3-4)

18 Nowhere to eat for a celebrity (7)

20 Oriental ruler making up the required measure (5)

45

ACROSS

1 Many drop – time for getting off the water (8)
5 Consolation is also perhaps given by the church (6)
9 Recovered and went through it all over again (8)
10 The minister has to have a meal around four (6)
11 Components made by employees in steel-works (8)
12 A six footer though not out of school (6)
14 Entered into an agreement and cut down (10)
18 Getting out more tonic maybe (10)
22 Blunders will reveal the defaulter in time (6)
23 Carol has got left inside for playing about (8)
24 Make some change in the current regulation (6)
25 Music composed without a note being written (8)
26 The Australian gardener? (6)
27 May be down on a winger (8)

DOWN

1 Wander about town (6)
2 An old soldier is more artful! (6)
3 A youngster found guilty of pinching? (6)
4 Protection for big cats – none may be trapped (10)
6 Relation possibly from the other side of the world (8)
7 This drink is put into a bag, note (8)
8 Day's end – flat time (8)
13 Taking some path meandering about composes the spirit (10)
15 Competent soldiers at first turned back (8)
16 Smart sailor in getting under way (8)
17 Jumble? It's cheap rubbish (8)
19 A painter rising before others to make check (6)
20 The abuse of one caught in traffic (6)

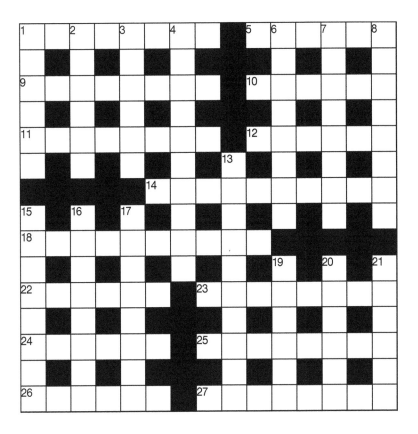

21 The monster in charge will get progressively worse (6)

46

ACROSS

1 Footballers here wealthier than management? (5,4,4)
10 A jolly group that identifies captain (7)
11 Mechanics' turning-point (7)
12 Calling for tax (4)
13 Rash in the colonies (5)
14 Who in France takes time to desert? (4)
17 Iverson turns out for Reading, say (7)
18 Picturesque presentation of slab of gold (7)
19 Whip kid, perhaps (7)
22 Maxim with dog in lead (7)
24 Popular Chinese leaders move very slowly (4)
25 20 make a point (5)
26 Message about low plant (4)
29 Capital, travelling first-class with Robin! (7)
30 Strivin' for an antipyretic? (7)
31 Backing-group in early European Song Contest (13)

DOWN

2 Cheeky pet from R Thames? (7)
3 Gin some put up (4)
4 Wall-builder suffered rain damage (7)
5 Echo with muse (7)
6 Jaunty rhythm in unusual *Il Trovatore* (4)
7 Nurse might run true to form? (7)
8 Invalid values, possibly, of people in variety (13)
9 No bread for these rounds? (7,6)
15 A great deal of vision (5)
16 Superior hearty on a half bottle? (5)
20 Place for records of principle American composer, not having succeeded (7)
21 Hear welcome? (7)
22 Hospital papers shredded, possibly (7)

23 Swell general fashion (7)
27 Yachting-centre, we hear, overawes people (4)
28 Take a second to nip back for a brisk drive (4)

47

ACROSS

1 Refrigeration firm's bankrupt stock? (6,6)
8 Presented to a minor journalist (7)
9 Clarify former scheme without one (7)
11 Mediocre senator suffers a breakdown (3-4)
12 A cripple home after World War II battle (7)
13 His sickness once caused recurrent disgust (5)
14 Expenditure on excursions (9)
16 Can a starter be produced in the kitchen? (3-6)
19 Brief summary about EU food policy (5)
21 Key conditions for producing properties (7)
23 Anything but poetic (7)
24 Homesteader who pays on the nail (7)
25 Fail to discharge (4,3)
26 Pioneer group with progressive political views? (7,5)

DOWN

1 Violent outburst after launch of distress signal (5-2)
2 In Cotswolds terminology, he's a gaffer (7)
3 Duck below the bedspread (9)
4 Knight entered region of conflict (5)
5 Parson made love to one of the choir (7)
6 Trained to arrange commercial transaction (5-2)
7 Epistolary scholar (3,2,7)
10 The loveliest rockery plant (4-2-6)
15 Arriving after negotiating mountain bends (7,2)
17 Scored by anyone but Edward (7)
18 A count in Pennsylvania may kneel on it (7)
19 Shot in the arm from both directions (7)
20 Hurried to serve small duck in Indian dish (7)
22 Glacial pinnacle causes terrible scare (5)

48

ACROSS

1 Details of problem suggest reducing staff as solution (5,3,7)
9 Opposed to profit, in a way (7)
10 In outskirts of Tewkesbury, wise woman is nervous (7)
11 Animal proverbially getting things back to front? (9)
12 Flynn seen in character role (5)
13 More than one reveals problems (7)
15 I let cat out – so touching (7)
17 Recounts taxes once squeezed the Spanish (7)
19 Hero finds Miss Moore a divine being (7)
21 Upset to miss start of public address (5)
23 Go with Bill to business (9)
25 Followed and changed direction, keeping right (7)
26 Intimidating, or sounding so to me (7)
27 London venue – called for one close to Victoria (5,6,4)

DOWN

1 Foreign money given to one's boy (7)
2 After tea, I run to seat (5)
3 Rigorous training here makes army officers pass out (9)
4 Unaffected by direction to cancel flat (7)
5 Strongly confirm, with most weight (7)
6 Man's speaking appearance (5)
7 Getting down details – one may have it taped (9)
8 Fine weather report – shade needed (3,4)
14 Not impressed with organ piece (9)
16 Dairy product parliamentarian fed to pet (9)
17 Nuclear plant creator redesigned (7)
18 Quickly look at boy, upset by disgrace (7)
19 Command to speak to recorder (7)

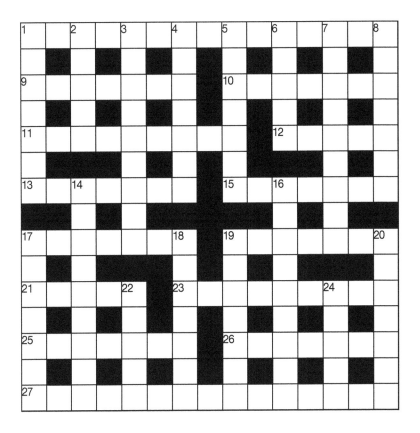

20 Well-ventilated cage in battery (3,4)
22 Peasant left to carry symbol of servitude (5)
24 Smell of a foreign capital (5)

49

ACROSS

1 Vegetable described in a newspaper cutting? (7)

5 T S Eliot play shows understatement (7)

9 Promises certain to be kept by a fool (7)

10 Many were carried away by it and lost their heads (7)

11 Chastise wanton whores with it (9)

12 He's good – and early! (5)

13 Quiet little person wants place for books (5)

15 About four hide, being reticent (9)

17 Changed circumstances may put a different complexion on it (9)

19 No head on the beer, that is strange (5)

22 A minor player makes more (5)

23 It's not alphabetical, that's obvious, of course (5,4)

25 Given a lift from this ode (7)

26 It gets down to sorting the list (7)

27 Depressed areas (7)

28 They are said to be just barren areas (7)

DOWN

1 Fruit dishes (7)

2 Husband substitute? (7)

3 Railwayman have points to look after (5)

4 Has to step out – fast! (9)

5 Drunk started smoking (3,2)

6 Watch and see how long the music takes (9)

7 Extremely important stations (7)

8 Gulpers out to get the whole hog (7)

14 RN fleet manoeuvre entertains mother in port (9)

16 Called without once becoming stuck-up (9)

17 Author to mark with a tick, say (7)

18 Rise for the workers? (3-4)

20 An early caller (7)

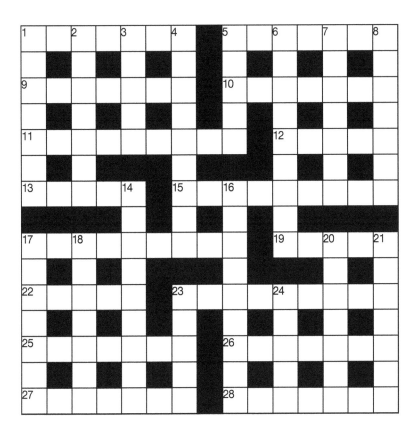

21 Train to be articulate (7)

23 Many poems need deciphering (5)

24 Loveless sailor staggers round bars (5)

50

ACROSS

6 Genuine worker to go and take this at the crossroads? (5-4,4)

8 Seafood, it sounds like beef (6)

9 Complete, despite the fact that alternative was included (8)

10 21s' pub? (3)

11 A doctor showed the way forward although was muddled (6)

12 Ten react badly during the interval (8)

14 Vacations when one's not at one's best (3-4)

16 Agree to speak favourably (7)

20 Go up possibly with new role for the introduction (8)

23 Refer to green poster first (6)

24 Might be blossom time (3)

25 Way he, (Ern), moved to an unspecified place (8)

26 Abrasive predicament? (6)

27 Not saving cash from one's personal allowance (8,5)

DOWN

1 Encourages a boy to make a vegetable dish (3,5)

2 Dolly, it's reacting in an unemotional way (8)

3 Sleeping colleague? (7)

4 Skilful Dora removed the article (6)

5 Gold in the air at dawn! (6)

6 Refreshment that's anything but a square meal! (5,2,6)

7 No answer! (8,5)

13 Blame the strike (3)

15 Trouble coming from a party (3)

17 Performs round yours truly, being sportive (8)

18 Clergyman always in distress (8)

19 Another needs to go round Middle Eastern estate (7)

21 Left by another way, the cockney lady's solicitor (6)

22 Being avaricious, rush in generally heartlessly (6)

51

ACROSS

1 Announce fantastic reduction (9)
9 The guy getting a note carried by raven (6)
10 Reviling a number making a row (9)
11 Decoration right on a king (6)
12 Having to do with making over in hard times (9)
13 Promise to settle on the quiet (6)
17 Some people are very serious, earnest and deep (3)
19 Regards money abroad as a bad thing (7)
20 Married ladies possibly get a questionable share-out (7)
21 Aim to cause annoyance (3)
23 Stout doorman (6)
27 Outstanding though mean worker (9)
28 Took things easy the Oriental way when in debt (6)
29 It just shows the pressure everybody's under! (9)
30 Transport and plant without cash (6)
31 Account for testament's crumpled appearance (9)

DOWN

2 Approached a raw beginner in dire straits (6)
3 Added comment about a marauder (6)
4 Like Hamlet and his uncertainty (6)
5 Ease only after study! (7)
6 A simple-minded healer (9)
7 Discontinue meetings of professional villains (9)
8 Put back control and come to a standstill (9)
14 Rate increase causing delay (9)
15 Soldiers forcibly recruited may well be subdued (9)
16 Go in and serve newly-appointed chief (9)
17 Ready for a party? (3)
18 In a beautiful dream youth meets girl (3)

22 Storm about a representative being upstanding (7)

24 Avoid responsibility for firm – up to collapse (3-3)

25 Running water supplied by master-builder (6)

26 An administrative fellow is from a South American range (6)

52

ACROSS

1 Firm keeping nothing in reserve (5)
4 Promises of parties in show ring (9)
8 Habit of university's first wise man (5)
9 Unexplained details of abandoned ambitions (5,4)
11 Musical soldier at the double? (4)
12 The French, mad dog is in the house (5)
13 Mighty blow, sending marbles back (4)
16 Giving grounds for Minnesota diet, possibly (13)
19 Old Bill's ferreting licence? (6,7)
20 Means of raising standard (4)
22 Cover for the van (5)
23 Size of a type of magpie? (4)
26 Slimmer does not want this order of set prayer (5,4)
27 Joke to work out (5)
28 Winning on the pools, is how he saw himself (9)
29 Turkey on a plate, to consume in feast (5)

DOWN

1 Pinched-looking old-timer? (4-5)
2 Continent admits wandering Angle, feeling no pain (9)
3 Reversible act (4)
4 Town memorably turning out cloth for overcoats (6,7)
5 Mid-off on field in a jumper! (4)
6 Strength of foreign wines (5)
7 Start attack (5)
10 Sanders supporting instrument of street-musicians (5-8)
14 Order of dice thrown over square (5)
15 Infidel has cooking-vessel lined with silver... (5)
17 ...baroque style makes it certain (9)
18 Recent fair game? (9)

20 James regularly taking the retriever (5)
21 Preside over church leaders' appearance (5)
24 House common in Home Counties, by motorway (4)
25 Tax no longer taken from discotheques (4)

53

ACROSS

1 Taking stock (11)
9 French fare for a politician in Connecticut (9)
10 Dress for a party with naval personnel (5)
11 Trinket from Bengal (6)
12 Nice beef stew appreciated by the vicar (8)
13 Where the worker looks for transportation cost? (6)
15 Most male ailments can be treated (8)
18 Maybe salt-and-water mixture is the answer (8)
19 Morning exam totally lacking in standards (6)
21 Quality goods (8)
23 Profit from China's disintegration (4,2)
26 Clear that cleric has retreated into sacred books (5)
27 Plenty to eat at the bakers' ball? (9)
28 Meeting fine lady with marriage in mind (6,5)

DOWN

1 Instrument used to make sherry, however (7)
2 This sultan was a huge fellow (5)
3 Hit by need of illumination (9)
4 Supporters produce payment on time (4)
5 Causing an obstruction on the road (2,3,3)
6 Good people gain God's favour (5)
7 Writer with depression found hanging (7)
8 Actor carrying explosive needs to act arrogantly (8)
14 What ramblers do for an easy win (4-4)
16 See large number of poets from Northern Italy (9)
17 Tony Carr resolved to be perverse (8)
18 Imagine taking drink with model (7)
20 Liberal organises English-Ulster meeting in fast time (7)
22 Bar from earliest opera by Handel (5)
24 Back high-class Brahman, maybe (5)
25 Go for a spin (4)

54

7 Talking to oneself, that's in character (9)

8 Tuck in one's clothes (5)

10 Socialist got off flight (4-4)

11 Die where current flows back in river (6)

12 Girl may seem mad, to some extent (4)

13 Dog races around churchyard (4,4)

15 Fourth district (7)

17 Pieces of cotton hardest to unravel (7)

20 Unashamed bombast by Iris (8)

22 Look – engineers are learning (4)

25 Samuel left a little food (6)

26 Ready money only, for fabric (8)

27 Request we rejected as out of line (5)

28 Wonderful thing doctor's given to one in need of food (9)

DOWN

1 Model problem (5)

2 One persecuted by two boys (6)

3 Select and anoint me, perhaps (8)

4 *The Case of the Burdened Traveller* (7)

5 Mistake over part of book causes delay (8)

6 Blonde has skilled job – smuggling (4,5)

9 Improve? Thousands die (4)

14 Good hand from capacity crowd (4,5)

16 Regret failing to keep one's record book (8)

18 Conceal problems within – one's not on the level, naturally (8)

19 Puzzled and rebellious, being arrogant (5,2)

21 Sally lost her first colleague (4)

23 Communist man held in detention (6)

24 Weeps, about to rise in confusion (5)

55

ACROSS

1 Mabel and I lurch if drunk – on this? (13)
10 A stubborn worker seen around a river vessel (7)
11 Caress a girl on the knee (7)
12 A song sung for joy (4)
13 A matter of extreme interest to the lender (5)
14 People go crazy running it (4)
17 Specifically used by diabetics (7)
18 No performance from one who behaves in an ostentatious manner (4-3)
19 Greet us, perhaps, with a wave? (7)
22 Foreign vessel is shrouded in silence (7)
24 Gratuity about right for the journey (4)
25 Put up with criticism (5)
26 Perhaps every term holds a recess (4)
29 Unnecessary warning to a caretaker? (7)
30 Save up for book (7)
31 Change sides? (5,3,5)

DOWN

2 Simpers, out to influence someone (7)
3 An exchange of blows, but there's nothing in it (4)
4 Catches, as one comes drunkenly home (5,2)
5 They decide if strikers are to be dismissed (7)
6 I turn to a matter of trivial importance (4)
7 Capital boom develops after depression (7)
8 Butt for the flower under the ha-ha (8-5)
9 Fifty-two knaves? (4,2,7)
15 Not in a whisper – permitted to be heard (5)
16 Dependable form of alloy (5)
20 Attack and capture (7)
21 Points to raise in a republic (7)
22 Pip took the dog in and tied it up (7)
23 I'm over the danger, though put in jeopardy (7)

27 Charitable sort (4)

28 Motoring organisation is held up on the continent (4)

56

ACROSS

1 Double-quick lifestyle devoted to pleasure and luxury (4-6)

6 Tooth, white when from London (4)

9 Certain four included were the most authoritative (10)

10 Vigour of brother before ten, it appears (4)

12 Left with your first musician (6)

13 It's to do with land, I hurried round Indian city first (8)

15 Rule not in the statute-book (9,3)

18 Steadily improving – or climbing? (2,3,2-3-2)

21 It restricts flight departures (8)

22 Make an error cause someone else's downfall (4,2)

24 Accustomed to being exploited (4)

25 Prolonged hesitation before I name the result (10)

26 Good-looking bowl? (4)

27 Shared gift however prudent (3,7)

DOWN

1 Like a violin requiring much dexterity? (6)

2 Expedition fair as could be (6)

3 Does a verbose judge give stiff punishment? (4,8)

4 Doctor gets round ban (4)

5 Guiding labourer, say, before imposing a curfew at college (10)

7 Dry area for taking off or landing? (8)

8 Does wrong (not right) surprisingly with the glad tidings (4,4)

11 Protecting metal box, keeping watch over it (12)

14 Support Turkish commander and another with biased information (10)

16 One cannot see why one might be stuck at the airport (8)

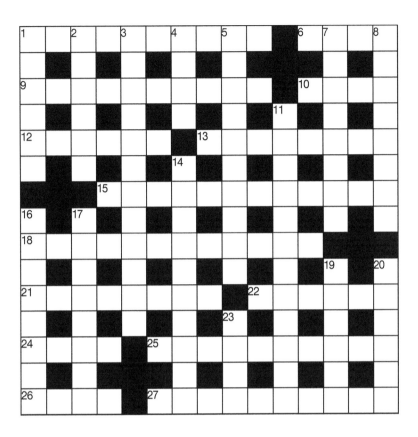

17 With no heavenly bodies in the cast! (8)

19 It is bound to keep a bone in place (6)

20 Supposed to have come from a shop in Edinburgh (6)

23 Head for the loch (4)

57

ACROSS

  1 Teenagers' allocation in rises (11)
  9 Underwear best the wrong way round – such a dilemma! (5,4)
10 Welsh leader the others twist (5)
11 Access taken here – of course (6)
12 Child hugging heart-broken furniture-designer (8)
13 He's too agitated to settle (6)
15 Declare a girl's put on weight (8)
18 A proposal to have nothing green at the riverside (8)
19 At some distance switches failed (6)
21 Horse-training for which groom needs time (8)
23 Like to include silver plant in the kitchen garden (6)
26 Revolutionary machinery, this! (5)
27 Roisterer – dreadful bully (9)
28 The smart secret agent's valet? (11)

DOWN

  1 Bill, having long hair, could be a player (7)
  2 Anything in a trough tempts swine (5)
  3 A ballet step from *The Trance* (9)
  4 Beats international sportsmen (4)
  5 Cutting in is not a feature, note (8)
  6 The seedsman swore to make a change (5)
  7 Concentrated – in time (7)
  8 Fine words! (8)
14 To peter out before a musical entertainment (8)
16 Sick of green? (3-6)
17 Conservatives getting bogged down panic! (8)
18 Businesslike but tender (7)
20 Most extreme letter written by a nuisance (7)
22 Possibly Myrtle and mum create friction (5)

24 She's just a little woman, it appears (5)
25 Provides means of defence for members (4)

58

ACROSS

1 All too human story in which evil makes a comeback (8)
9 Treat raw spillage seen in the river (5,3)
10 Slight quarrel with father in the street (4)
11 Goes ahead and plays the star part (5,3,4)
13 Drink from the basin (8)
15 Anne's going out with North Polar explorer (6)
16 Guns return, this animal may be hunted (4)
17 One can't imagine being without them (5)
18 They look and sound agreeable (4)
20 Unethical perfume brought back by pupil (6)
21 Status symbols? (8)
23 Adjustment in damages (12)
26 Knock back a portion of gin (4)
27 Sad pair evicted initially, having gone wrong here (8)
28 Carefully examines any seals broken (8)

DOWN

2 A word of twenty-six letters (8)
3 Have a great time – never mind the tears! (3,6,3)
4 A well-filled vessel (6)
5 Sheep to handle, we hear (4)
6 Works of art produced from scratch (8)
7 Bank of Scotland (4)
8 Apprentices the boss sent sprawling (8)
12 The country's top people emerging from Heathrow? (6,6)
14 Emile provides something fragrant (5)
16 The main picture (8)
17 Lilo is in decomposed state (8)
19 Travel overseas to get home (8)

22 A bad mark for the errant magistrates lacking rebuke (6)

24 Indicate a suitable victim (4)

25 Time to return to a region (4)

59

ACROSS

1 It's fine leather for the head's family! (8)
5 Act One must be revised without delay (2,4)
9 Music tolerated when flying (8)
10 Walk some way with unsteady gait (6)
12 An area capable of yielding (9)
13 Possibly ten royal characters are to register (5)
14 Land reversing the Spanish Italian agreement (4)
16 A yarn may well be spun about such a staff (7)
19 Writing a book about one's break up (7)
21 To drop a quarter would appear prudent (4)
24 A slice of brawn – it really needs salt (5)
25 Learn of reformed cheat's despair (9)
27 Drink imbibed by a woman doctor (6)
28 A beast holding a number back is just not fair (8)
29 Shop at break for this stuff (6)
30 Changed direction and caused some irritation (8)

DOWN

1 Sings for the workers after church (6)
2 Left a local leader to make an entrance (6)
3 Feeling the pinch, but not for long (5)
4 "Far from the madding crowd's —— strife" Gray's *Elegy* (7)
6 Note the call for exercising restraint (9)
7 Twelve – and not one on time (8)
8 Increased by five hundred following general appraisal (8)
11 Accommodation for the services (4)
15 Pusillanimous invertebrate (9)
17 The market for chessmen? (8)
18 An undertaking to tighten up (8)
20 Repeat a little gift of soft-centre chocolates (4)
21 Flighty creature responsible for disputes (7)

22 Stop showing spirit (6)
23 The man left in bed to be observed (6)
26 Opinion that's backed up just the same (5)

60

ACROSS

1 On Friday, anything makes one tense (7)
5 Give up hope of being wildly praised (7)
9 The best a few find offensive (7)
10 A revolt is occurring (7)
11 Book of stamps? (5)
12 I am in hospital, fretting (9)
13 Dissertations about universal Greek hero (7)
14 Ken and lady writhing in the nude (7)
16 Talked about having headgear (7)
19 Spinster is game (3,4)
22 Unexpected test for measles? (4,5)
24 Get together my confession of stupidity (5)
25 In summary, it's unpopular to queue (7)
26 More spacious per item repacked (7)
27 Toyed absent-mindedly with violin? (7)
28 Unfamiliar way to the mountains (7)

DOWN

1 I get close, within foot, of painting (4,3)
2 Can I be friendly? (7)
3 In poor motels, I go very miserable (9)
4 Worst possible place to refuel car? (3,4)
5 Showing no emotion as late nap disturbed (7)
6 Change dress (5)
7 Flavouring has a Belfast origin (7)
8 Socialists wouldn't govern so fairly (7)
15 One abducting child taken to head (9)
16 Clear the stage – prepare to sail (4,3)
17 A daughter chose to be separated from parents (7)
18 Out of one's depth here in river – wait (4,3)
19 Not the Shetlands, nor Skye, surprisingly (7)

20 Middle Easterner had a lot of night's entertainment (7)

21 Merit of French verse in translation (7)

23 Cold: I'll put central heating on (5)

61

ACROSS

1 South Thamesside area that's changing (8)
5 Getting explosive about drink as a gift (6)
9 Stagger as a result of shots in a disturbance (8)
10 A country hat (6)
12 Offer from a caretaker? (6)
13 Walk around one's heavenly garden (8)
15 A European wants poultry with no stuffing (7)
16 The leading man in the Roman legions (4)
20 Bringing to notice an odious fellow (4)
21 Money invested in London? (7)
25 In this locality conservationists appear essential (8)
26 Deal with food summary (6)
28 Ladies' fashion models (6)
29 Act natural – for the present (8)
30 The Jewish quarter got the orders (6)
31 Fly from ordeal with utmost speed (8)

DOWN

1 Writing up star parts is a pain! (6)
2 Temporary thespian work (6)
3 Depend, or maybe that's what's thought (8)
4 A small number don't talk but eat (4)
6 A base with an oil-refining place (6)
7 Fell back bored when questioned (8)
8 Exploits a rodent's potential (6,2)
11 Court dress? (7)
14 A drug of oceanic derivation (7)
17 The purpose of the match is coming out (8)
18 Accountants' aspiration – only the finest suiting (8)
19 Such banter can get hurtful in time (8)
22 Band around a member (6)

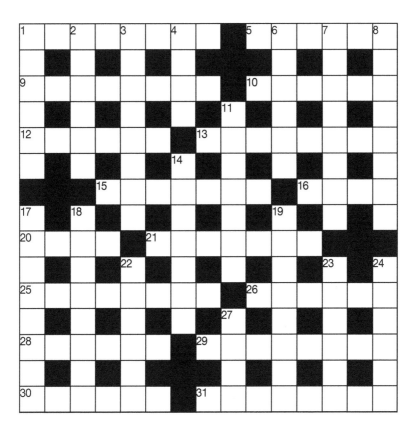

23 About to go over the border to live (6)
24 In spring this tree transforms a road (6)
27 Sound charge (4)

62

ACROSS

1 Defective tense (9)
9 Poet's always following vehicle in his way through life (6)
10 Outlaw in favour of journalist (9)
11 Quite beautiful? (6)
12 Unorthodox monarch we find in dailies (9)
13 African political party – any turning out? (6)
17 The main subject of Elgar's pictures (3)
19 Their mounts can be spoiled by post-impressionists! (5,10)
20 Social occasion for a queen, perhaps (3)
21 Strongly urge one to take part in Essex horticultural membership (6)
25 I'd go back to reading for amusement (9)
26 A sweetheart passionately aroused (6)
27 If backing carpeting, make it safe from 26! (9)
28 Driving nail obliquely – eg into bend (6)
29 Winning final holds attention (9)

DOWN

2 Swampy planet, hot to unknown degree (6)
3 English deciphering runes, in effect (6)
4 Loud quarrel to produce litter (6)
5 What offers choice of channels is close – inevitable, possibly? (5,10)
6 Switch musical number (9)
7 Shelter of Alice's intended, despatched before rail-strike (6-3)
8 Artist escaping from city arson (9)
14 No repeats, unusually, in this unnatural language (9)
15 Cut – longer established feature of the Oval (9)
16 A piece intended, say, to be in A flat? (9)

17 Shed tears in Caesar's obituary (3)
18 Trouble reported with drink? (3)
22 Be in awe of Longfellow's rider (6)
23 After centre-court, more certain he will take too much of the interest (6)
24 Companies' merger arranged in secure place (6)

63

ACROSS

1 Nurses eat stew and wine (9)
9 Most unusual means of departure (3-3)
10 A humorous show gets Home Counties backing, anyway (2,2,5)
11 Last month a legislator had to vamoose (6)
12 Model trustee admits he is a torchbearer (9)
13 Suit needed by gardeners (6)
17 Pat is an expert (3)
19 Ideal lady-love in the Orient (7)
20 A graduate don ordered to beat it (7)
21 In Lucknow a riotous mob caused conflict (3)
23 Encouraged, despite failure at the rodeo! (6)
27 Foe in fact displayed fond feelings (9)
28 Within 24 hours doctrine caused consternation (6)
29 Force prisoners to exercise (9)
30 Gradually destroys 'is lady's poems (6)
31 Supervise bringing the stall across (5,4)

DOWN

2 A couple of Poles given first aid (6)
3 Stagger around on seeing an adder (6)
4 Change of editor caused uproar (6)
5 Hand-picked painter portrays Greek princess (7)
6 Proposition to forge an entry ticket (4,1,4)
7 Fight and row alternately? (3,3,3)
8 Make way for favourites to back a team (4,5)
14 Chancellor's strategy to settle huge debt on time (3,6)
15 Cocaine is stolen by a marksman (5,4)
16 Coastguard who always salts away some cash (4-5)
17 Fall on a cold night (3)
18 Local restriction (3)

22 Indignity for African coalition (7)
24 Leslie and his lad have class (6)
25 Sound system to transplant trees by mid-October (6)
26 Reason I have abbreviated French term first (6)

64

ACROSS

1 Receiving bill, go white in appearance (6)
4 False incentive to take promissory notes (8)
10 Port is the deepest, regularly (9)
11 A number nearby (5)
12 Brandy-glass at children's party? (7)
13 Distance a marine goes to give support at sea (4-3)
14 Police led to drug in wood (5)
15 Agree end will be horrible for traitor (8)
18 No actors available for *Robinson Crusoe*? (8)
20 Disruptive trumpeter who's left the band? (5)
23 No mountainous regions produce these fruits (7)
25 Food for insect including fruit (7)
26 Separate beds for brothers perhaps (5)
27 Valuable picture almost red after restoration (3,6)
28 Organs joined in harmony, as one sees (3-2-3)
29 Bird's place includes new tree (6)

DOWN

1 Retreat as American autumn returned (4,4)
2 Primrose subdues impudence (7)
3 Unscrupulous hedonists come to grief (9)
5 Proof I work with *Windows* – so simple to control (5,2,2,5)
6 Governor helps one to go straight (5)
7 Where to grow fruit or vegetable (7)
8 August, when melons grow wild (6)
9 Spirited march goes on, though this is gravely decaying (4,6,4)
16 Develop a regiment's organisation (9)
17 Kissed, say, using mouth muscle (8)
19 Greed for processed caviare... (7)
21 ...for the bigger Greek consumer (7)

22 Courage – one's hit by drinker (6)
24 Blast! Nothing for enjoyment! (5)

65

ACROSS

1 Great at organising water sports (7)
5 New issue stamp on letter is entrusted to him (7)
9 Manage valley by a system of holding land (7)
10 Wrong terrain for a coach (7)
11 Reserves high place for publications (9)
12 An air of sadness (5)
13 Not qualified to give the final figure (5)
15 It may help to rescue a country from mad policy (9)
17 Well-rounded notes in an unbeatable score (4,5)
19 Tony's knocked out by infamous world champion (5)
22 Fifty-one doctors appear to be members (5)
23 Head of state needs trip abroad (9)
25 Desert folk struggle to succeed (3-4)
26 Officer in uniform or overall (7)
27 Infuriates with fresh demands (7)
28 Screen has red centre and unusual rose edging (7)

DOWN

1 Not a well cooked portion of savoury (7)
2 Vessel that shoots over the waves (7)
3 Some Spartans return with snares (5)
4 A great man in history (9)
5 Part of flower-plate design (5)
6 Is noticeably not flush? (6,3)
7 Marconi's resort? (7)
8 Where children may go between two and five (7)
14 It cuts down the light coming from headlamps (9)
16 Not a driver to overtake on green, perhaps (9)
17 A vital point when it comes to a purchase (7)
18 Restricted cover includes free time (7)

20 Cut some grain in an outhouse (7)
21 Annoys with stinging words? (7)
23 The Fleet Street crowd (5)
24 Victor, out West, is a pretty good shot (5)

66

ACROSS

1 Matter Joe exchanged with dancing girl (9)
6 Tout losing one of his rights to become a shopkeeper (5)
9 Pity unfortunate state representative (7)
10 Some tobacco trace I get removed (9)
11 Witty saying about magpie right to be included (7)
12 It is not good, having a duty to write it off (3,4)
13 Be punctilious but stick with less than one ritual (5,2,8)
18 Woolly account of the heart (7)
20 Roman historian understood us (7)
22 Delete as industrial action is forbidden (6,3)
23 Dance-ed (7)
24 Turn in short publication about Biblical king (5)
25 S in place of ZO with sudden emphasis when dealing with notes (9)

DOWN

1 Smart set providing basis for one in retirement (8)
2 Camellia troubled Jo in a cap (8)
3 Builder losing his head to a clergyman (6)
4 Left copper in hat with this perfumed powder (6)
5 Match fit (8)
6 Resent having to ask for charity, urged otherwise (8)
7 Singer that lets off steam (6)
8 Relax one's severity again before Easter (6)
14 Eating partner? (8)
15 Colin has become a new man (8)
16 Had become too big for his boots? (8)
17 Answer that's only 50 per cent correct (3,3,2)
18 Usual way of having trade (6)
19 Full of enthusiasm and sense of urgency to go? (6)

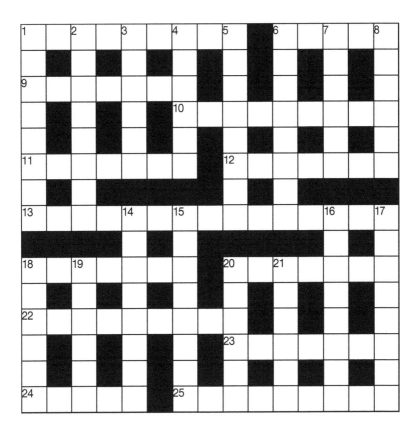

20 Do some needlework and make lace also (6)

21 Chapter head had sound suggestions for the cloth (6)

67

ACROSS

1 Models deem breaks intrusive (10)
6 Car hired for a team of irregulars? (4)
10 Scots can not get this tropical plant (5)
11 Very green gregarious type (9)
12 Street guide for the foreigner (8)
13 Put off some women with crude terminology (5)
15 Wild flower to be seen round the North (7)
17 Scene calling for ten in stage presentation (7)
19 Characteristic consideration (7)
21 He'll put a good finish on wooden furniture (7)
22 Popular place to feed in (2-3)
24 Herb's got two girls (8)
27 Men hope an error can be found, but they're exceptional (9)
28 Nobody has caught cold – for the present (5)
29 Figure one's accomplished (4)
30 Such dealers get no rest. It's a mistake (10)

DOWN

1 Debunk the synthetic (4)
2 Cheat lots of people out of gifts (9)
3 Making money in Britain, owns a place abroad (5)
4 Keeping the Latin Quarter in view is an artful trick (7)
5 Grew older, dull, and awfully rude (7)
7 Likely holding of Parisian expert (5)
8 Form relatively close personal ties (10)
9 Pass a portion that's really liberal (8)
14 Went down and gave a very generous gratuity (10)
16 Support demonstration (8)
18 Confidence man's profession? (9)
20 Nothing but one river in another river makes a rushing stream (7)

21 Far from cool (7)
23 Groom about to be committed to prison (5)
25 Among mixed fruit (5)
26 Not all little troubles seem minor (4)

68

ACROSS

6 First bogeyman, say? (3,6,4)
8 Acid to assist blind farmhouse victims (6)
9 Fifi acts to reform base, cowardly fellows (once) (8)
10 Henry to retire? That's new! (3)
11 Goddess armed from the outset, at that time, in two acres (6)
12 Flat old hat? Correct! (8)
14 Detailed popular measure (2-5)
16 School of minor surgery (7)
20 Not easily moved over bad route (8)
23 Complaint of youth in springtime (6)
24 Greek character met in your holidays (3)
25 Georgia's airy source of Victorian brilliance? (8)
26 Dried fruit is getting wet (6)
27 Glad aeroplane is refurbished for writer of stories (5,5,3)

DOWN

1 Queen visiting Empire, possibly, for the first night (8)
2 Lying on arms, can't contain cry of pain (8)
3 Cot made up in back of nuclear plant (7)
4 Sticking to rules, having some gastric trouble (6)
5 Twins, for example, reversing small car (6)
6 Photographing dense undergrowth from estate-car (8-5)
7 Sinister control in Rome, possibly? (4-4,5)
13 Single game point (3)
15 Standard power on a river (3)
17 A jolly college, we hear, of heraldry (8)
18 Muse, a variety of lilac almost in bloom (8)
19 Filter out quarter of what is fruit-bearing (7)
21 Liquid lost in purposeful lager production (6)
22 Nettles in sausages with head cut off (6)

69

ACROSS

1 Billy is fat (6)
4 Presumptuous idiot gets stylish Chinese porcelain (8)
9 To promote feelings of sympathy is arrogant (6)
10 Biased couple accommodating rowing crew (8)
12 Communicants receive it at mass (4)
13 An attractive young woman is easy to catch (5)
14 Lighter produced by firm in Devon (4)
17 Making excellent progress as a blacksmith (7,5)
20 An importer so disturbed that he takes off (12)
23 Sounds like genuine Iranian currency (4)
24 Prepared for rainy weather in Burgundy (5)
25 Wild dog returned from the stream (4)
28 Orangeman's endless audacity! (8)
29 Is an attorney allowed to leave the country? (6)
30 Scratching a living (8)
31 Skater managed to go hell for leather (6)

DOWN

1 Removal of fox's tail leads to rebuff (5-3)
2 Records attempt to produce ornamental fabric (8)
3 The finest estate houses noble Italian family (4)
5 Practise dramatic plagiarism to outshine others (5,3,4)
6 A craving, for instance, rugby players rejected (4)
7 International law is unaffected (6)
8 Leave university function in a long dress (2,4)
11 Church members go on creating mayhem (12)
15 Letter a thousand American soldiers sent back (5)
16 Pass out when feeling dizzy (5)
18 What market traders pay for everything in the coach (8)
19 Return of lottery proves a disadvantage (8)

21 Golly! Someone's hacked at the bread! (6)
22 He forbids others to show the flag (6)
26 A six-footer used to be quiet (4)
27 Shy band of players (4)

70

ACROSS

1 Italian island produce shows a sign of winter (9)
8 Musical representation of aimless rebels (3,10)
11 Duty to which criticised people are taken (4)
12 Feeble Rector goes in to die (5)
13 Sunhat, the best one (4)
16 In prison, see our fortitude (7)
17 Divorced wife with more than enough warning (7)
18 Wild animal cruelly chained (7)
20 Good firm engaging fool as painter (7)
21 Not complete, but a hopeful state (4)
22 Run into tour going round city (5)
23 Astonish by returning crazy (4)
26 Cloth-worker has important rank (8,5)
27 These days, take exam in very distressing circumstances (9)

DOWN

2 With which a Cockney wounds? (4)
3 Again supply book (7)
4 Concern to guard container for rifle (7)
5 Polish unknown gem (4)
6 Information published on rogue whales in Australia (3,5,5)
7 Two-note piece of music? What rot! (13)
9 Mick upset horribly by armed robbers' demand (5,2,2)
10 Extremely rigid Conservative heading for place of concealment? (9)
14 First two letters from Hywel are useful (5)
15 Striker chosen for game (5)
19 Extent of imperial land? (7)
20 Mineral – it is used in fires (7)
24 Ancient gives silver to boy (4)
25 Under stress, being instructed orally (4)

71

ACROSS

1 Soldiers put to flight? (10)
9 Release when no charge is made (4)
10 Christian virtue fills a need, somehow (4-6)
11 International group is performing in concert (6)
12 Put out in unusual transport (7)
15 Some skyscraper turbulence can upset (7)
16 Give way under pressure (5)
17 Measure taken to indicate marriage relations (4)
18 Travel authority is located in Virginia (4)
19 Appears to understand the manuscript (5)
21 Ring-fighter? (7)
22 Frenzied Norse warrior (7)
24 Drank up a round behind the others (6)
27 Ten on trial perhaps – for being racialist? (10)
28 Sent to restore a bird sanctuary (4)
29 Acts for, concerning gratuities (10)

DOWN

2 Abraham Lincoln, to start with, was murdered (4)
3 Pretend to have influence (6)
4 Critical stage of increasing gravity for spacemen (2-5)
5 Bespectacled greeting in American state (4)
6 Kissed perhaps – the usual start between girl and boy (7)
7 Maintain a good atmosphere in the air force (10)
8 It enabled Queen Victoria to stick to her post (5,5)
12 Like gremlins, be mischievous (10)
13 Delightful move by a footballer in a difficult position? (6,4)
14 Duck down (5)
15 Born under Victoria, true (5)
19 At least he's private (7)

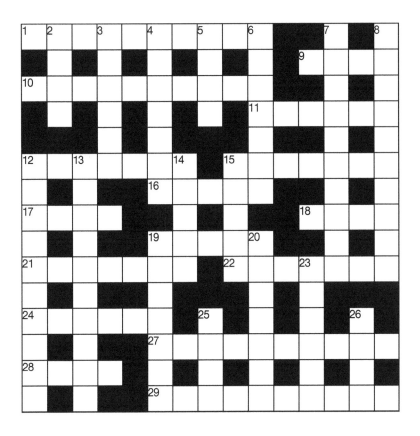

20 South-eastern town of France is actually in Spain (7)

23 In panic a hundred became hard to find (6)

25 Prevent pots getting knocked over (4)

26 The speed of a flier (4)

72

ACROSS

1 Inherit dubious coin tome (4,4)
5 A loose woman? (6)
10 More or less using unpolished phrases (7,8)
11 Toy had finally been soundly shaken (7)
12 Disposed of old money Derek returned full of holes (7)
13 Endlessly confuse left and right possible being contemptuous (8)
15 It's impossible going forwards or backwards (3,2)
18 Search for that French saint (5)
20 I started out after all the others (8)
23 High level correspondence (7)
25 Mystic interpretation of why the taxi is by Welsh lake (7)
26 Impartially despite girl's eagerness at city (15)
27 Had correspondence at the end (6)
28 I leave another direction for a place in Devon (8)

DOWN

1 Remedy included a recipe for poison (6)
2 Has to have pain, there's nothing in it that's right under one's nose (9)
3 Breathing apparatus at home for Alan shortly in her grasp (7)
4 Edward took Joy in without Jack and played in an idle way (5)
6 Daniel afterwards removed a gun from an East African (7)
7 Warble until first robin comes in (5)
8 Needing a smashing Swiss resort (8)
9 Diamond set off in November (8)
14 Belief in necessity of delivering mail fast (8)
16 Will have a statement of beliefs (9)

17 Blue waste (8)
19 Eat another loaf or scone (7)
21 Batting table, it's found inside the ship (7)
22 Is able, in the distance, to find a gorge (6)
24 Rough artist went ahead of the foreign agent (5)
25 Number of sheets reportedly for singers (5)

73

ACROSS

7 Stock limitation (6,3)
8 A protective surface can be inapt (5)
10 Many people see right through him! (8)
11 Tries to catch crooks (6)
12 Enchanting creature gaining a little experience (4)
13 No tea given, oddly enough (8)
15 Looking for a fixer around Ireland (7)
17 Reduction of capital growth (7)
20 The odd person taking drugs (8)
22 Backing friends, makes a hit (4)
25 School of agriculture? (6)
26 Gut reaction shown this month in court (8)
27 Awfully eager to arrange match (5)
28 Servicemen calling for some relaxation (9)

DOWN

1 Pleased to find beastly food about 2p (5)
2 If rest is disturbed there's controversy (6)
3 Concerned with seeing a change for the better (8)
4 Member holding an unopened tin that's bent (7)
5 Left the queen without anything for amusement (8)
6 Try to scoff about a two points lead (9)
9 A supporter, note, can be biting (4)
14 Get a new set back with unbridled anger (9)
16 An instrument of the law? (8)
18 Making a craft doubly popular, he's killing! (8)
19 Original artist adopting Oriental clothes (7)
21 Pop's soft beard (4)
23 It's mad, mad, being in the centre (6)
24 A player in a most satisfactory position (5)

74

ACROSS

1 A role that is distinct (5)
4 Heavens! Business enterprise meant to go broke! (9)
8 Strains of Harrow school's opening (5)
9 Centre in which adolescents stick together? (5,4)
11 Standard quarter-cut (4)
12 Light meal for number in bed (5)
13 Heavenly body like Madonna? (4)
16 Eve, maturing, turned out contentious (13)
19 Oldie taking higher subject (6,7)
20 French duke goes to king for nothing (4)
22 Gold sovereign? (5)
23 Fare from France (by rail, that is) (4)
26 Fickle person slices up each lemon (9)
27 Strong stuff from England's openers in bad light (5)
28 Barking people require such a leg-protector (4-5)
29 Wise to leave wild edelweiss in city (5)

DOWN

1 What tourists see in Athens – a harvest on poor soil (9)
2 Confirm Cartesian plan (9)
3 In which to see expert bowling analysis? (4)
4 Contraption of magnificent fellow, in the air? (6,7)
5 Looking pale? Take a shot! (4)
6 Conspicuous effect of city area, almost at the last minute (5)
7 Underground right for such a plant? (5)
10 Insured, can not come to harm – that's natural (13)
14 Gleaming silver common? (5)
15 Cereal one kept in labyrinth (5)

17 Blissful state of innocence (9)
18 Hide outside? (9)
20 Adorns ship's platforms (5)
21 Film I made of South American animal (5)
24 Composer in rubber gloves (4)
25 Party in the Italian image (4)

75

ACROSS

1 First bid is the final offer of course (8,5)
10 It spells death to make peace with America (7)
11 Begin to sing out of doors (4,3)
12 Should it always include marines? (4)
13 Some money for a pen (5)
14 Blast! That's a set-back (4)
17 Somehow her suit gets covered in hairs (7)
18 A cheese of unusually high standing? (7)
19 Maybe toxin extracted from gentian (7)
22 Mum's getting dear Italian make-up (7)
24 Continue to look back (4)
25 Foul stench caused a furore (5)
26 Examination of gold and aluminium (4)
29 Girl takes time setting it in mosaic (7)
30 I translated a Latin language (7)
31 Enduring labour whilst imprisoned (2,11)

DOWN

2 Time serving hairdresser (7)
3 Estimate what the current price is (4)
4 Stocked up at the supermarket (2,5)
5 Justification for acquiring land (7)
6 Regretted being utterly uncivil (4)
7 Bead-moulding placed initially in holiday home (7)
8 Game instruction to the Vice Squad (6,7)
9 Having little luck at sketching (7,1,5)
15 Expulsion of enemies was Pride's first impulse (5)
16 Resin used to tint the hair (5)
20 A tenor's awful betrayal (7)
21 Yes, indeed! Make mine a pint! (3,4)
22 He goes to Jerusalem to get a fine house (7)
23 Uppity doughboy in Scottish island put on trial (7)
27 Lead in the Roman army (4)
28 Ultimate prize within one's grasp (4)

76

ACROSS

1 Shares a room and has a big laugh (7,2)
8 Straining to hear – projection's falling (13)
11 Whisky, a production of island (5)
12 Unstable mountains? (5)
13 Members of band run into singer (5)
16 Anti-gravity? (6)
17 Brave girl finally dropped addictive drug (6)
18 From Essex, I leave for life abroad (5)
19 Translated verses from China (6)
20 A very lucky and most competent... (6)
21 ...pole with pointy head that's offensive (5)
24 Alchemist has a small work team (5)
26 Regiments' fans (5)
27 Accepts a rally is possible from these footballers (7,6)
28 Dreadfully sectarian sort of logic (9)

DOWN

2 The last letter one had from Athens (5)
3 If successful he gets a lot knocked down (6)
4 Book flight from Egypt (6)
5 Superior pep-pill? (5)
6 Don't speak now – the audience is plastered (5,4,4)
7 Secondary consequence of fly-half's fumble? (5-2,6)
9 His work is full of administrative errors (9)
10 One may be in a state after he makes a pass (9)
13 Anoint head of bishop with smaller quantity (5)
14 Sensitive, like Molly Malone's cockles? (5)
15 Cut off second try (5)
22 Fussy scholar adds page to version of Dante (6)
23 Fit in notices for changes (6)

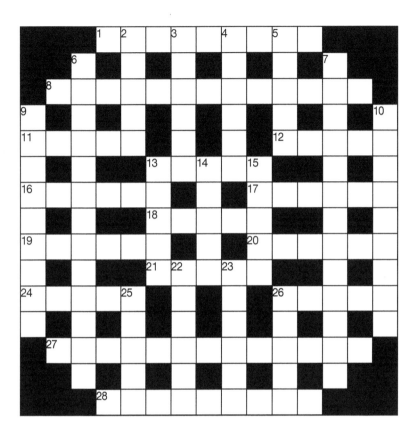

25 Opera to look at briefly? Almost (5)
26 Bring up a chunk of wood (5)

77

ACROSS

1 Music for church service (3,5)
9 Vegetarian, bright-eyed and bushy tailed (8)
10 Land set back by a lake (4)
11 Useless demonstration of hunger-marchers? (5,7)
13 Mistakes appear once fuss is made (8)
15 Quickly put the balance in the Post Office (6)
16 Irritation Ken gets in the kitchen (4)
17 Breaks for a card-game on board (5)
18 Feed a mouse some cheese (4)
20 It's natural in staple food, we hear (6)
21 Society match? (8)
23 The number of the hospital? (12)
26 The net gain from trawling (4)
27 Girl embraces chap back in Hamlet's place (8)
28 Bad comedian was diabolical (8)

DOWN

2 How one's stomach may feel with liver not in order? (2,6)
3 Acquit, but without costs (4,2,6)
4 Raise drink after drink, result – uproar! (6)
5 Some rules Pythagoras had to observe (4)
6 Your pegs are hammered –and these attached (3-5)
7 Composer and arranger being oddly selective (4)
8 Stand often taken by public speakers (8)
12 Instantly, but not here and now (5,3,4)
14 Post workers! (5)
16 Takes off meat, it is cooked (8)
17 Crime publication not for northern readers (8)
19 A word of praise (8)
22 I'm about to stay in the same place (6)
24 Swap services around in church (4)
25 Made to last (4)

78

ACROSS

1 Resent having to accept the second said thing that does not follow the general rule (4,9,2)

9 What, say, flower was uprooted by birds swimming? (9)

10 Have only a fraction of a body of constables (5)

11 Do something accommodating again (7)

12 A live TV broadcast in Israel (3,4)

13 Regret being cruel at heart (3)

14 Fellow with Sally 'e intercepted wrongly (7)

17 Fit in the German inhabitant (7)

19 Cap that is not worn on one's head (7)

22 The romp round a place in Northumberland (7)

24 The French article in the open country (3)

25 Term Lee devised for a tall plant (3-4)

26 It is possible to calm down the queen in the story (7)

28 Fare needed to board a bus perhaps (3,2)

29 Sound as a bell (4-1-4)

30 Move clumsily with a pair of like measures (4,3,4,4)

DOWN

1 Powerful tug that can be relied on (5,2,8)

2 Drawing all but the top of the boat (5)

3 Along the way in France? (2,5)

4 Falsify accounts with fifth rate lines, it's done in the kitchen (7)

5 Guided polite members to front door (7)

6 Sudden decision of one Frenchman on the beat (7)

7 Dandy serf not in music city (9)

8 Intoxicated cox? (3,4,3,5)

15 Left one composing motet outside before four with recurring theme (9)

16 Lady from Long Island going to mid-Wales (3)
18 Try to win affection in court (3)
20 Title a Brontë could have arranged (7)
21 Most of the charged particle used on the printing plate (7)
22 Coat for baby in afternoon performance (7)
23 Batter some of the defence (7)
27 Main water supply (5)

79

ACROSS

1 An isolated community lives without scandal (9)
9 Proof the head should carry rifle (7)
10 Bad accident caused by many a mum in drink (5-2)
11 Do the crossword again for 8 (7)
12 Plain-spoken with depressed Tories (9)
14 A pen responsible for the big hold-up in Egypt (5,3)
15 Have a fling, taking in a show (6)
17 Chaste characters needing money to get a bag (7)
20 Representative? A member scoffed (6)
23 Appearance of coppers round about head of state (8)
25 Letters written as a priest perhaps (9)
26 He will no longer play Shylock (7)
27 May be completely taken in! (7)
28 Re-unite possibly to make the train (7)
29 Nobody up? No comment (9)

DOWN

2 Not a particular individual (7)
3 Reason for strengthening attachment? (7)
4 Woman doctor out of order in America (8)
5 Pleasurable activities for good losers (6)
6 The law enforcer does make a list (9)
7 Told about everything in verse (7)
8 Fix and check and explosive device (9)
13 The man's shown around at church but comes out (7)
15 A demonstration of scorn for fruit (9)
16 Insisting upon reform is strange (9)
18 Serving the Spanish with wrong mineral in Hamlet's castle (8)
19 This might well be a target for sailing folk (7)

21 Measured the little Greek with a double (7)
22 Ramblers gain support here (7)
24 Calling for private transport always (6)

ACROSS

1 Some token dalliance here in Lakeland gateway (6)

4 Hot tempered woman, one of the few in the second row (8)

9 Coin fashionable to utter (6)

10 Pinches bits (8)

12 Properly fit, fortunately (4)

13 Fireplace relatively large, we hear (5)

14 Silver on tin is a problem (4)

17 Sailor transported and looked after, faraway (6-6)

20 Hindmost name, possibly, in carpeting (12)

23 A woman always at a distance (4)

24 Inert form of saltpetre (5)

25 Track of marsh bird (4)

28 German team-leader turned out nice? (8)

29 Suffer punishment with a sherry-glass (6)

30 Is one put up in the garden for dippers and divers? (8)

31 Strode around the county (6)

DOWN

1 Fair Isle, perhaps, for king taking a winter trip (8)

2 Joyce, for example, has consort of ten viols (8)

3 Italian flower of particular note (4)

5 Treated patient in Rye is cooler (12)

6 Row makes retired fellow healthy (4)

7 Man is, notwithstanding Donne's statement (6)

8 Flag officer? (6)

11 This gymnast almost trip in twist? (12)

15 A lyric poem in a terminal (5)

16 The Anglo-French concoction causes amnesia (5)

18 Was it tossed by Romans in rained-off states? (8)

19 Beefy law-breaker in *Genesis*? (8)

21 Label on tin shows Cambridge origin? (6)
22 He puts a price on Virginia's troubled rule (6)
26 Company doctor's curry (4)
27 Bird dead with nothing to follow? Same again? (4)

ANSWERS

1

Across
1 Face to face
6 Pale
9 Water-melon
10 Cold
13 Minaret
15 Nailed
16 Rafter
17 Pull the other one
18 Remind
20 Fisher
21 Gelatin
22 Veda
25 Magistrate
26 Lino
27 Pennyroyal

Down
1 Fawn
2 Cute
3 Torrid
4 Free association
5 Clover
7 Apostrophe
8 Elderberry
11 On approval
12 Silly mid-on
13 Meeting
14 Taken in
19 Debase
20 Fitter
23 Navy
24 Reel

2

Across
1 Ballot-paper
9 Relocated
10 Ad hoc
11 Itched
12 Scotsman
13 Rebate
15 Priority
18 Gossamer
19 Fennel
21 Momentum
23 Fright
26 Liner
27 Talkative
28 End of the day

Down
1 Barrier
2 Lilac
3 Orchestra
4 Path
5 Pedicure
6 Riant
7 Hackney
8 Champion
14 Basement
16 Overreach
17 Rebutted
18 Gymslip
20 Lithely
22 Nerve
24 Grind
25 Clef

3

Across
1 Exactor
5 Chapter
9 Enraged
10 Dubbing
11 Impatient
12 Lathe
13 Easel
15 Sternness
17 Pressures
19 Eager
22 Scene
23 Landgrave
25 Enamour
26 Imagine
27 Spectre
28 Lodgers

Down
1 Eremite
2 Apropos
3 Tight
4 Redresser
5 Cadet
6 Ambulance
7 Thistle
8 Regress
14 Lashes out
16 Essential
17 Possess
18 Elevate
20 Granite
21 Reefers
23 Larne
24 Grand

4

Across
1 Bubble and squeak
9 Harbour
10 Siamese
11 Neil
12 Doubt
13 Sari
16 Turn out
17 Nest egg
18 Elapses
21 Proviso
23 Cast
24 Court
25 Skid
28 Négligé
29 Bellini
30 Slip of the tongue

Down
1 Behind the scenes
2 Barrier
3 Loom
4 Airport
5 Dustbin
6 Quay
7 Elevate
8 Keeping good time
14 Boost
15 Ascot
19 Assegai
20 Soonest
21 Parable
22 Inkling
26 Kilo
27 Alto

5

Across
1 Noted
4 Spanking
10 Abolish
11 In a spot
12 Maid
13 Strap
14 Vain
17 Sign of the times
19 Get one's own back
22 Plan
23 Spuds
24 Keen
27 Whither
28 Eyesore
29 Dynamite
30 Sweep

Down
1 Near miss
2 Tooting
3 Do in
5 Private soldier
6 Neat
7 In place
8 Get on
9 That's the spirit
15 Donor
16 Ninny
18 Skin-deep
20 Elation
21 Acerose
22 Pawed
25 Whim
26 Keys

6

Across
6 Head over heels
8 Mascot
9 Republic
10 Hoe
11 Stripe
12 Abnormal
14 Craning
16 Bar-code
20 Harangue
23 Samson
24 Act
25 Circular
26 Hold it
27 Grit one's teeth

Down
1 Sanction
2 Northern
3 Retreat
4 Chopin
5 Member
6 Heart-breaking
7 Spit and polish
13 Oar
15 Inn
17 Aesthete
18 Cameleer
19 Learned
21 Archie
22 Gallop

7

Across
1 Major issue
9 Nero
10 Ventilator
11 Appeal
12 Covered
15 Vermeer
16 Dared
17 Nark
18 Cast
19 Bends
21 In a word
22 Instead
24 Eluded
27 Accomplice
28 Cram
29 Los Angeles

Down
2 Amen
3 Obtuse
4 Ill-used
5 Site
6 Enraged
7 Decelerate
8 Collar-stud
12 Confidence
13 Vernacular
14 Dated
15 Verdi
19 Bradawl
20 Snowman
23 Twelve
25 Aces
26 Acne

8

Across
1 Husband and wife
9 Marital
10 Syncope
11 Rung
12 Caerphilly
14 Clench
15 Blissful
17 Fastener
18 Mental
21 At a stretch
22 Crib
24 Briefed
25 Thought
26 Electric heater

Down
1 Homeric
2 Springer-spaniel
3 Ante
4 Dallas
5 Nostrils
6 Winchester
7 From left to right
8 Jekyll
13 Scientific
16 Defender
17 Flabby
19 Lobster
20 Acetic
23 Bode

9

Across
1 Love-story
9 Aspire
10 Certainty
11 Wither
12 Adventure
13 Enamel
17 Add
19 Sets off
20 Regards
21 Try
23 Resign
27 Carnation
28 Neared
29 Dining-car
30 Evader
31 Stag party

Down
2 Overdo
3 Esteem
4 Twists
5 Retired
6 Espionage
7 Nightmare
8 Heartless
14 Estranges
15 Stash away
16 Roughened
17 Aft
18 Dry
22 Realist
24 Ending
25 Stigma
26 Hobart

10

11

12

13

Across
1 First offender
10 Needles
11 Nourish
12 Crab
13 Agile
14 Pump
17 Oddment
18 Barge in
19 Tubular
22 Lion-cub
24 Upas
25 Spume
26 Diet
29 Channel
30 Nominal
31 Compressed air

Down
2 Ireland
3 Sold
4 On sight
5 Fan club
6 Nous
7 Epicure
8 Knock-out punch
9 Ship in a bottle
15 Jelly
16 Groom
20 Bravado
21 Repulse
22 Laments
23 Chianti
27 Snap
28 Amid

14

Across
1 Juliana
5 In depth
9 Concordat
10 Basal
11 Pleat
12 Spearhead
13 Tarpaulin
16 Tasty
17 Bathe
18 Bow-window
20 Spindrift
23 Gesso
25 Divan
26 Automatic
27 Surname
28 Hayloft

Down
1 Jackpot
2 Lance
3 About-face
4 Andes
5 In the know
6 Debar
7 Possessed
8 Holiday
14 Retriever
15 Lubricate
16 Thingummy
17 Besides
19 Woodcut
21 Donna
22 Titch
24 Set to

15

Across
1 Caches
4 Serenata
9 Mashie
10 Stopcock
12 Eden
13 Legal
14 Erin
17 Chiropractor
20 Sixth-formers
23 Pear
24 Bored
25 Lima
28 Converge
29 Nepali
30 Discrete
31 Nestor

Down
1 Commerce
2 Cosmetic
3 Emit
5 Entrance fees
6 Espy
7 Aboard
8 Asking
11 Merrythought
15 Solid
16 Board
18 Hesitant
19 Espalier
21 Spaced
22 Vaunts
26 Peer
27 Mere

16

Across
1 Frances
5 Bent
9 Second-class mail
10 Flea
11 Limit
12 Wrap
15 Let down
16 Grimace
17 Seaweed
19 Bassets
21 Grit
22 Flute
23 Full
26 Over-development
27 Wear
28 Sprouts

Down
1 Fistful
2 Ancient Mariner
3 Cone
4 Section
5 Bearing
6 Nose
7 Eclipse
8 Marriage bureau
13 Bower
14 First
17 Signore
18 Deliver
19 Battles
20 Salutes
24 Edge
25 Spur

17

Across
1 Blazing the trail
9 Orleans
10 Logging
11 Dive
12 Bobby
13 Abel
16 Yorkist
17 Trapeze
18 Popover
21 Brought
23 Ajar
24 Stash
25 Blue
28 Isolate
29 Octette
30 Generating plant

Down
1 Broadly speaking
2 All over
3 Imam
4 Gosport
5 Halibut
6 Togs
7 Amiable
8 Legal settlement
14 Sieve
15 Manor
19 Platoon
20 Retreat
21 Bassoon
22 Galatea
26 Fair
27 Stop

18

Across
1 Play hard to get
7 Fatal
8 Bonaparte
9 In force
10 Hangers
11 Gully
12 Spectator
14 Back-pedal
17 Depot
19 Nervous
21 Risotto
22 Favourite
23 Obese
24 Tender-hearted

Down
1 Pitiful
2 Allergy
3 Ranch
4 Topknot
5 Garment
6 Treasure trove
7 Fringe benefit
8 Blessed
13 Enlarge
15 Caravan
16 Produce
17 Disport
18 Pithead
20 Swish

19

Across

 1 Half-brother
 9 Non-runner
10 Mould
11 Floats
12 Flat-iron
13 Let off
15 Tribunal
18 Absolute
19 Stay up
21 Lipstick
23 Rocket
26 Tutti
27 Carthorse
28 First eleven

Down

 1 Handful
 2 Lento
 3 Bountiful
 4 Oink
 5 Heraldry
 6 Remit
 7 Ordinal
 8 Currency
14 Tosspots
16 Betrothal
17 Stock car
18 All-star
20 Pattern
22 Thief
24 Kirov
25 Trot

20

Across

 1 Incog
 4 Ripcords
 8 Hen-party
 9 Sanction
11 Tardier
13 Evening up
15 Time is on our side
18 Reclaimed
21 Scrappy
22 Ringside
24 Calabria
25 Honolulu
26 Hades

Down

 1 In hot water
 2 Centrism
 3 Gladioli
 4 Rhys
 5 Chichi
 6 Riding
 7 Sion
10 Adenoids
12 Reformed
14 Pretty pass
16 Reproach
17 Inspired
19 Canton
20 Abseil
22 Rash
23 Ecru

21

Across

 1 Shut off
 5 Repasts
 9 Adeptly
10 Buoyant
11 Dirt cheap
12 Eerie
13 Lehar
15 Go half-way
17 Alligator
19 Romeo
22 Ought
23 Open-ended
25 Netball
26 Atelier
27 Sheikhs
28 Retread

Down

 1 Scandal
 2 Unearth
 3 Optic
 4 Flyweight
 5 Rub up
 6 Propeller
 7 Sparrow
 8 Satiety
14 Right back
16 Horsehair
17 Amounts
18 Legatee
20 Midwife
21 Ordered
23 Ogles
24 Erect

22

Across
1 Batsman
5 Go round
9 Cambridge
10 Vista
11 Larne
12 Regarding
13 Gospeller
16 Got at
17 Humus
18 Waywardly
20 Crossbred
23 Duple
25 Lie to
26 Adjourned
27 Retrace
28 Notched

Down
1 Backlog
2 Tamer
3 Murderess
4 Nadir
5 Glengarry
6 Rover
7 Unstinted
8 Draught
14 Somnolent
15 Lower-case
16 Grand-aunt
17 Heckler
19 Yielded
21 Stoma
22 Dijon
24 Pinch

23

Across
1 Storksbill
9 Trio
10 Astringent
11 Earned
12 Tooting
15 Gallant
16 Green
17 Used
18 Etna
19 Stout
21 Hospice
22 Swindon
24 Thalia
27 Temporally
28 Noel
29 Heaven-sent

Down
2 Test
3 Rarest
4 Sinking
5 Item
6 Lateran
7 Transacted
8 Goods-train
12 Touchstone
13 Overstates
14 Grate
15 Genus
19 Scratch
20 Twosome
23 Nomads
25 Emma
26 Clan

24

Across
1 Smattering
6 Bore
9 Later
10 Signorina
12 Change-ringing
14 The blues
15 Atonal
17 Casing
19 Bloomers
21 Stone the crows
24 In the main
25 Ingot
26 Lard
27 Advertiser

Down
1 Sell
2 Autocue
3 Turn a blind eye
4 Resigned
5 Niger
7 Opinion
8 Evangelist
11 Ornithologist
13 Stock-still
16 Alicante
18 Shooter
20 Ensigns
22 Hoard
23 Stir

25

Across

1 Stiff upper lip
10 Unravel
11 Regular
12 Leak
13 Holds
14 Oman
17 Condole
18 Doggone
19 Tabloid
22 Topical
24 Keep
25 Canoe
26 Onus
29 Yew-tree
30 Tornado
31 Expert opinion

Down

2 Terrain
3 Five
4 Unloose
5 Paraded
6 Rage
7 In limbo
8 Duplicate keys
9 Orange-blossom
15 Motor
16 Agape
20 Bees-wax
21 Dialect
22 Two-step
23 Centavo
27 Free
28 Wren

26

Across

1 Trappist
9 Old story
10 Chic
11 Trouble afoot
13 Corridor
15 Dorado
16 Amah
17 Nizam
18 Sikh
20 Thrust
21 Refrains
23 Under control
26 Ivan
27 Sargasso
28 Kilogram

Down

2 Rehoboam
3 Picture-house
4 Inroad
5 Tomb
6 Addendum
7 Dodo
8 Eye-tooth
12 Forestalling
14 Razor
16 Altruism
17 Notecase
19 Kinshasa
22 Formal
24 Dark
25 Nook

27

Across

7 Backwash
9 Editor
10 Aden
11 Drawing pin
12 Unison
14 Exchange
15 Coarse
17 Nestor
20 Landrace
22 Caress
23 Second-rate
24 Cant
25 Dinner
26 Evensong

Down

1 Sardonic
2 Akin
3 Garden
4 Mediocre
5 Ringmaster
6 Coming
8 Healer
13 Standpoint
16 Standard
18 Resonant
19 Relate
21 Averil
22 Crewel
24 Cosh

28

Across
1 Oxtail
4 Headlamp
9 Expose
10 Stair-rod
12 Loot
13 Peony
14 Peru
17 Accomplished
20 Unfavourable
23 Earn
24 Shady
25 Fund
28 Vanguard
29 Estate
30 Scottish
31 Recess

Down
1 Overload
2 Top-notch
3 Inst
5 Eat ones words
6 Drip
7 Air-bed
8 Podium
11 Aeolian harps
15 Amend
16 Heard
18 Obdurate
19 Heedless
21 Delves
22 Bronco
26 Just
27 Isle

29

Across
1 Insider
5 Classes
9 Evening
10 Explain
11 Aspirates
12 Raise
13 Error
15 Orphanage
17 Posthaste
19 Noose
22 Scrub
23 Stippling
25 Toe-nail
26 Inspire
27 Dynasty
28 Grained

Down
1 Iterate
2 Stepper
3 Drier
4 Righteous
5 Clegs
6 Appertain
7 Stamina
8 Sincere
14 Rehoboams
16 Presiding
17 Posited
18 Surgeon
20 Opinion
21 Egghead
23 Sally
24 Pasta

30

Across
1 Pull a fast one
8 Augusta
9 Stilted
11 Draught
12 Singles
13 Valve
14 Euphrates
16 Retractor
19 Maple
21 Implore
23 Satsuma
24 Transit
25 Tillage
26 Sliding scale

Down
1 Pigtail
2 Lasagne
3 Apartment
4 Asses
5 Thinner
6 Notelet
7 Hand over fist
10 Disaster area
15 Parasites
17 Topsail
18 Aroused
19 Matilda
20 Plumage
22 Eaten

31

Across
6 Pepper and salt
8 Crater
9 Friction
10 Eli
11 Beef up
12 Steerage
14 Adulate
16 Erudite
20 Scot free
23 Visits
24 Roe
25 Allergic
26 Thieve
27 Restaurant car

Down
1 Spiteful
2 Decrepit
3 Raffish
4 Advice
5 Captor
6 Perpendicular
7 Thought it over
13 Emu
15 Alf
17 Riveting
18 Distinct
19 Mercury
21 Theism
22 Rag-day

32

Across
1 Improper
6 Sprite
9 Maggot
10 Sinister
11 Crotchet
12 Course
13 Thoroughfare
16 Monkey-puzzle
19 Twined
21 Retitled
23 Grooming
24 Everso
25 Heifer
26 Tiresome

Down
2 Meagre
3 Right
4 Pet theory
5 Risotto
6 Sonic
7 Reshuffle
8 Treasure
13 Taking off
14 Gazetteer
15 Got worse
17 Upright
18 Jetsam
20 Drier
22 Tress

33

Across
1 Seawards
5 Scares
9 Altruist
10 Margin
11 Contempt
12 Smells
14 Wellington
18 Exasperate
22 Sketch
23 Relevant
24 Aplomb
25 Opposite
26 Ending
27 Agitated

Down
1 Scarce
2 Antony
3 Abused
4 Disappears
6 Charming
7 Regulate
8 Singsing
13 Clothes-peg
15 Persuade
16 Labelled
17 Spaceman
19 Set out
20 Lariat
21 Attend

34

Across
1 Jude the Obscure
9 Cast-off
10 Sniffle
11 Pile
12 Friendless
14 Tackle
15 Decipher
17 Sidecars
18 Starch
21 Phenomenal
22 Topi
24 Enslave
25 Aileron
26 Understatement

Down
1 Jackpot
2 Displaced person
3 Tool
4 Effort
5 Besieged
6 Childbirth
7 Refresher course
8 Teaser
13 Electorate
16 Creepers
17 Sapper
19 Hairnet
20 Cabana
23 Blue

35

Across
1 Hemisphere
6 Abut
9 Canon
10 Lampshade
12 Volume of trade
14 Northern
15 Kibosh
17 Nectar
19 Craggier
21 Plenty of space
24 Roundworm
25 Grand
26 Darn
27 Point taken

Down
1 Hack
2 Miniver
3 Single-hearted
4 Hallmark
5 Romeo
7 Bravado
8 There there
11 Sitting target
13 Uninspired
16 Freshman
18 Chequer
20 Icepack
22 Ovolo
23 Odin

36

Across
1 Commissionaire
9 Live it up
10 Tamil
12 Amos
13 Passing out
15 Keepsake
16 Cinema
18 Umpire
20 Declutch
23 Shetlander
24 Sign
26 Lying
27 Flat iron
28 Store detective

Down
2 Moidore
3 Iced
4 Setbacks
5 Oppose
6 Aston Villa
7 Rumpole
8 Slot machine
11 Jack Russell
14 Astrologer
17 Relevant
19 Predict
21 Tripoli
22 Knifed
25 Zinc

37

Across
1 Waste paper
9 Mete
10 Spider's web
11 Evolve
12 Dowsers
15 Acronym
16 Tiara
17 Site
18 Stun
19 Rebel
21 Jurymen
22 Learned
24 Cliché
27 Water-melon
28 Echo
29 Light verse

Down
2 Alps
3 Tidies
4 Purport
5 Pawn
6 Rebecca
7 Wellington
8 Determined
12 Disc jockey
13 Watertight
14 Siren
15 Ariel
19 Renewal
20 Leveret
23 Revere
25 Stag
26 Boos

38

Across
1 Support
5 Roasted
9 Thorn
10 Kitchener
11 Fishmonger
12 Echo
14 United States
18 Estrangement
21 Noes
22 Standstill
25 Gastropod
26 Atlas
27 Redoubt
28 Elector

Down
1 Set off
2 Proust
3 Ornamental
4 Taken
5 Rotterdam
6 Ashy
7 Tenacity
8 Dormouse
13 Stony stare
15 Tight spot
16 Teenager
17 Stressed
19 Violet
20 Closer
23 Nudge
24 Frau

39

Across
1 Sidecar
5 Apropos
9 Overact
10 Coterie
11 Posit
12 Amendment
13 Realist
14 Shelter
16 Sapient
19 Work out
22 About turn
24 Hotel
25 Trident
26 Scourge
27 Righter
28 Poke out

Down
1 Stopper
2 Deep-sea
3 Coastline
4 Retract
5 Archers
6 Rated
7 Portent
8 Swelter
15 Earthwork
16 Shatter
17 Probing
18 Truster
19 Winds up
20 Ontario
21 Tallest
23 Treat

40

Across
1 Parasite
5 Coupon
9 Reporter
10 Warren
12 Seaman
13 Bargains
15 Leaflet
16 Alec
20 Lope
21 Revelry
25 Instance
26 Tobago
28 Teaser
29 Steering
30 Reeves
31 Fanlight

Down
1 Perish
2 Replay
3 Streaked
4 Tier
6 Orange
7 Particle
8 Nonesuch
11 Tapered
14 Offence
17 Cloister
18 Apostate
19 Arboreal
22 Raceme
23 Paring
24 Nought
27 Etna

41

Across
1 Hard core
5 Offset
9 Milliner
10 Redcap
12 Look after
13 Homer
14 Scar
16 Sporran
19 Car park
21 Cosy
24 Drawl
25 Number one
27 Around
28 All in all
29 Netted
30 Atherton

Down
1 Homily
2 Roll-on
3 China
4 Re-enter
6 Fleshpots
7 Sycamore
8 Tapering
11 Ares
15 Challenge
17 Acid rain
18 Break out
20 Kind
21 Camelot
22 Pop art
23 Fell in
26 Elite

42

Across
1 On the house
9 Bust
10 Fly-by-night
11 Rabbit
12 Knowing
15 Esparto
16 Grant
17 Sofa
18 Give
19 Bison
21 Moisten
22 Withers
24 Keeper
27 Door-to-door
28 Tack
29 Dotted line

Down
2 Nile
3 Hebrew
4 Hanging
5 Urge
6 Entrust
7 Humberside
8 Stationers
12 Kiss Me Kate
13 Off-licence
14 Grain
15 Endow
19 Bearded
20 Nightie
23 Handel
25 Colt
26 Worn

43

Across

6 Maid of all work
8 Assist
9 Dramatic
10 Due
11 Maxima
12 Straight
14 Channel
16 Chemist
20 Escapade
23 Sentry
24 Amp
25 Staysail
26 Inroad
27 Smoking jacket

Down

1 Division
2 Post-date
3 Hardest
4 Altair
5 Somali
6 Massachusetts
7 Knights errant
13 Ace
15 Nap
17 Hospital
18 Mandrake
19 Sea-legs
21 Anyhow
22 Acacia

44

Across

1 Companionship
7 Folly
8 Punctilio
9 Excerpt
10 Chicago
11 Idyll
12 Evergreen
14 Gunpowder
17 Fence
19 Elusive
21 Layette
22 Threading
23 Abbot
24 Running battle

Down

1 Colicky
2 Mayoral
3 Ionic
4 Nothing
5 Haldane
6 Pronouncement
7 Feeling better
8 Pithead
13 Earplug
15 Neutron
16 Origami
17 Fly-past
18 Notable
20 Eking

45

Across

1 Drainage
5 Solace
9 Recapped
10 Divine
11 Elements
12 Insect
14 Contracted
18 Extraction
22 Errata
23 Sporting
24 Switch
25 Serenade
26 Digger
27 Feathers

Down

1 Darwen
2 Archer
3 Nipper
4 Greatcoats
6 Oriental
7 Anisette
8 Eventide
13 Atmosphere
15 Reversed
16 Starting
17 Pastiche
19 Arrest
20 Tirade
21 Ogress

46

Across
1 White Hart Lane
10 Armband
11 Fulcrum
12 Duty
13 Hives
14 Quit
17 Version
18 Tableau
19 Leather
22 Proverb
24 Inch
25 Score
26 Flax
29 Nairobi
30 Aspirin
31 Meistersinger

Down
2 Hamster
3 Trap
4 Hadrian
5 Reflect
6 Lilt
7 Nurture
8 Vaudevillians
9 Amateur boxing
15 Sight
16 Abbot
20 Archive
21 Receive
22 Perhaps
23 Enlarge
27 Cows
28 Spin

47

Across
1 Frozen assets
8 Awarded
9 Explain
11 One-star
12 Alamein
13 Leper
14 Outgoings
16 Tin-opener
19 Recap
21 Estates
23 Inverse
24 Settler
25 Give out
26 Advance party

Down
1 Flare-up
2 Oldster
3 Eiderdown
4 Arena
5 Soprano
6 Trade-in
7 Man of letters
10 None-so-pretty
15 Turning up
17 Notated
18 Patella
19 Reviver
20 Cursory
22 Serac

48

Across
1 Facts and figures
9 Against
10 Twitchy
11 Carthorse
12 Errol
13 Several
15 Tactile
17 Relates
19 Demigod
21 Annoy
23 Accompany
25 Tracked
26 Awesome
27 Royal Albert Hall

Down
1 Francis
2 Chair
3 Sandhurst
4 Natural
5 Fattest
6 Guise
7 Recording
8 Sky blue
14 Voluntary
16 Camembert
17 Reactor
18 Scandal
19 Dictate
20 Dry cell
22 Yokel
24 Aroma

49

Across

1 Parsnip
5 Litotes
9 Assures
10 Tumbrel
11 Horsewhip
12 Prior
13 Shelf
15 Secretive
17 Chameleon
19 Eerie
22 Extra
23 Clear soup
25 Hoisted
26 Thistle
27 Valleys
28 Deserts

Down

1 Peaches
2 Reserve
3 Nurse
4 Posthaste
5 Lit up
6 Timepiece
7 Termini
8 Splurge
14 Fremantle
16 Conceited
17 Chekhov
18 Ant-hill
20 Rooster
21 Express
23 Codes
24 Rails

50

Across

6 Right-hand turn
8 Mussel
9 Thorough
10 Inn
11 Addled
12 Entr'acte
14 Off-days
16 Approve
20 Prologue
23 Advert
24 May
25 Anywhere
26 Scrape
27 Spending money

Down

1 Egg salad
2 Stolidly
3 Partner
4 Adroit
5 Aurora
6 Round of drinks
7 Negative reply
13 Rap
15 Ado
17 Playsome
18 Reverend
19 Demesne
21 Lawyer
22 Greedy

51

Across

1 Introduce
9 George
10 Maligning
11 Oberon
12 Recession
13 Plight
17 Sea
19 Eyesore
20 Misdeal
21 Try
23 Porter
27 Important
28 Rested
29 Barometer
30 Sledge
31 Statement

Down

2 Neared
3 Raider
4 Danish
5 Console
6 Herbalist
7 Prorogues
8 Reinstall
14 Temporise
15 Repressed
16 Sovereign
17 Set
18 Amy
22 Rampant
24 Cop-out
25 Stream
26 Andean

52

Across

 1 Hoard
 4 Manifesto
 8 Usage
 9 Loose ends
11 Gigi
12 Lodge
13 Swat
16 Sedimentation
19 Search warrant
20 Jack
22 Front
23 Pica
26 Spare tyre
27 Crack
28 Narcissus
29 Treat

Down

 1 Hour-glass
 2 Analgesia
 3 Deed
 4 Melton
   Mowbray
 5 Flea
 6 Sinew
 7 Onset
10 Organ-grinders
14 Edict
15 Pagan
17 Intricate
18 Newmarket
20 Jason
21 Chair
24 Semi
25 Scot

53

Across

 1 Shoplifting
 9 Camembert
10 Adorn
11 Bangle
12 Benefice
13 Towage
15 Manliest
18 Solution
19 Amoral
21 Property
23 Cash in
26 Overt
27 Abundance
28 Paying court

Down

 1 Sackbut
 2 Osman
 3 Lamplight
 4 Feet
 5 In the way
 6 Grace
 7 Pendent
 8 Domineer
14 Walk-over
16 Lombardic
17 Contrary
18 Suppose
20 Lenient
22 Estop
24 Hindu
25 Turn

54

Across

 7 Soliloquy
 8 Pleat
10 Left-wing
11 Expire
12 Emma
13 God's acre
15 Quarter
17 Threads
20 Flagrant
22 Lore
25 Morsel
26 Cashmere
27 Askew
28 Humdinger

Down

 1 Poser
 2 Victim
 3 Nominate
 4 Luggage
 5 Slippage
 6 Fair trade
 9 Mend
14 Full house
16 Register
18 Hillside
19 Stuck up
21 Ally
23 Remand
24 Cries

55

Across
1 Liebfraumilch
10 Ampoule
11 Patella
12 Glee
13 Usury
14 Amok
17 Insulin
18 Show-off
19 Gesture
22 Spanish
24 Trip
25 Stick
26 Apse
29 Caution
30 Reserve
31 Heads and tails

Down
2 Impress
3 Bout
4 Reels in
5 Umpires
6 Iota
7 Colombo
8 Laughing-stock
9 Pack of thieves
15 Aloud
16 Loyal
20 Seizure
21 Estonia
22 Secured
23 Imperil
27 Kind
28 Asia

56

Across
1 Fast-living
6 Fang
9 Definitive
10 Brio
12 Lyrist
13 Agrarian
15 Unwritten law
18 On the up-and-up
21 Birdcage
22 Trip up
24 Used
25 Indecision
26 Dish
27 Far sighted

Down
1 Fiddly
2 Safari
3 Long sentence
4 Veto
5 Navigating
7 Airfield
8 Good news
11 Safeguarding
14 Propaganda
16 Fogbound
17 Starless
19 Splint
20 Opined
23 Ness

57

Across
1 Adolescents
9 Tight spot
10 Wrest
11 Entrée
12 Sheraton
13 Soothe
15 Announce
18 Overture
19 Afield
21 Dressage
23 Lovage
26 Rotor
27 Terrorise
28 Bondservant

Down
1 Actress
2 Ought
3 Entrechat
4 Caps
5 Notching
6 Sower
7 Intense
8 Sentence
14 Operetta
16 Off-colour
17 Frighten
18 Orderly
20 Deepest
22 Shrub
24 Anita
25 Arms

58

Across

1 Fallible
9 Water rat
10 Spat
11 Takes the lead
13 Absinthe
15 Nansen
16 Stag
17 Ideas
18 Eyes
20 Amoral
21 Insignia
23 Compensation
26 Trap
27 Paradise
28 Analyses

Down

2 Alphabet
3 Let things rip
4 Bucket
5 Ewes
6 Etchings
7 Brae
8 Students
12 Landed gentry
14 Elemi
16 Seascape
17 Illinois
19 Emigrate
22 Stigma
24 Mark
25 Area

59

Across

1 Capeskin
5 At once
9 Airborne
10 Stroll
12 Tractable
13 Enter
14 Isle
16 Spindle
19 Atomise
21 Sage
24 Nitre
25 Heartache
27 Healer
28 Brunette
29 Potash
30 Switched

Down

1 Chants
2 Portal
3 Short
4 Ignoble
6 Tethering
7 Noontide
8 Enlarged
11 Pews
15 Spineless
17 Pawnshop
18 Contract
20 Echo
21 Sparrow
22 Scotch
23 Beheld
26 Tenet

60

Across

1 Fraught
5 Despair
9 Noisome
10 Arising
11 Album
12 Impatient
13 Theseus
14 Nakedly
16 Chatted
19 Old maid
22 Spot check
24 Amass
25 Outline
26 Emptier
27 Fiddled
28 Strange

Down

1 Fine art
2 Amiable
3 Gloomiest
4 The pits
5 Deadpan
6 Shift
7 Aniseed
8 Rightly
15 Kidnapper
16 Cast off
17 Adopted
18 Deep end
19 Orkneys
20 Arabian
21 Deserve
23 Chill

61

Across
1 Swapping
5 Talent
9 Astonish
10 Panama
12 Tender
13 Paradise
15 Genoese
16 Hero
20 Toad
21 Capital
25 Inherent
26 Digest
28 Ideals
29 Donative
30 Ghetto
31 Fleetest

Down
1 Smarts
2 Acting
3 Pondered
4 Nosh
6 Abadan
7 Examined
8 Trades on
11 Lawsuit
14 Cocaine
17 Striking
18 Cashmere
19 Badinage
22 Armlet
23 Reside
24 Street
27 Toll

62

Across
1 Imperfect
9 Career
10 Proscribe
11 Pretty
12 Charwomen
13 Libyan
17 Sea
19 Stamp collectors
20 Bee
21 Exhort
25 Diversion
26 Aflame
27 Fireproof
28 Toeing
29 Endearing

Down
2 Marshy
3 Ensure
4 Farrow
5 Cable television
6 Hairpiece
7 Sentry-box
8 Crayonist
14 Esperanto
15 Gasholder
16 Apartment
17 Sob
18 Ale
22 Revere
23 Usurer
24 Cocoon

63

Across
1 Sauternes
9 Way-out
10 As it comes
11 Decamp
12 Usherette
13 Spades
17 Dab
19 Heroine
20 Abscond
21 War
23 Bucked
27 Affection
28 Dismay
29 Constrain
30 Erodes
31 Stand over

Down
2 Assist
3 Totter
4 Rioted
5 Electra
6 Make a pass
7 Box and cox
8 Step aside
14 The budget
15 Crack shot
16 Life-saver
17 Dew
18 Bar
22 Affront
24 Lesson
25 Stereo
26 Motive

64

Across
1 Facade
4 Spurious
10 Lowestoft
11 Local
12 Balloon
13 Yard-arm
14 Copse
15 Renegade
18 Castaway
20 Rogue
23 Oranges
25 Aliment
26 Twins
27 Old master
28 Eye-to-eye
29 Petrel

Down
1 Fall back
2 Cowslip
3 Dishonest
5 Putty in my hands
6 Ruler
7 Orchard
8 Solemn
9 John Brown's body
16 Germinate
17 Pectoral
19 Avarice
21 Greater
22 Bottle
24 Gusto

65

Across
1 Regatta
5 Postman
9 Rundale
10 Trainer
11 Bookstall
12 Dirge
13 Total
15 Diplomacy
17 Full marks
19 Tyson
22 Limbs
23 President
25 Rat-race
26 General
27 Maddens
28 Reredos

Down
1 Rarebit
2 Gunboat
3 Traps
4 Alexander
5 Petal
6 Stands out
7 Minorca
8 Nursery
14 Lampshade
16 Passenger
17 Fulcrum
18 Limited
20 Sheared
21 Nettles
23 Press
24 Inner

66

Across
1 Majorette
6 Baker
9 Typical
10 Cigarette
11 Epigram
12 Bad debt
13 Stand on ceremony
18 Cardiac
20 Tacitus
22 Strike out
23 Tangoed
24 Magog
25 Sforzando

Down
1 Mattress
2 Japonica
3 Rector
4 Talcum
5 Eligible
6 Begrudge
7 Kettle
8 Relent
14 Drinking
15 Nicholas
16 Outgrown
17 Yes and no
18 Custom
19 Raring
20 Tattoo
21 Chintz

67

Across
1 Meddlesome
6 Taxi
10 Canna
11 Extravert
12 Stranger
13 Deter
15 Violent
17 Diorama
19 Respect
21 Dresser
22 In-put
24 Rosemary
27 Phenomena
28 Nonce
29 Done
30 Stationers

Down
1 Mock
2 Donations
3 Lhasa
4 Sleight
5 Matured
7 Adept
8 Intermarry
9 Handsome
14 Overtipped
16 Election
18 Assurance
20 Torrent
21 Distant
23 Preen
25 Mango
26 Less

68

Across
6 Sir Robert Peel
8 Formic
9 Caitiffs
10 Hot
11 Athena
12 Outright
14 In-depth
16 Lancing
20 Obdurate
23 Malady
24 Rho
25 Gaslight
26 Raisin
27 Edgar Allan Poe

Down
1 Première
2 Couchant
3 Reactor
4 Strict
5 Gemini
6 Shooting-brake
7 Left-hand drive
13 Run
15 Par
17 Armorial
18 Calliope
19 Fertile
21 Ullage
22 Angers

69

Across
1 Butter
4 Assuming
9 Uppity
10 Weighted
12 Host
13 Dolly
14 Scow
17 Forging ahead
20 Impersonator
23 Rial
24 Macon
25 Flow
28 Mandarin
29 Canada
30 Scraping
31 Streak

Down
1 Brush-off
2 Tapestry
3 Este
5 Steal the show
6 Urge
7 Intact
8 Go down
11 Congregation
15 Sigma
16 Faint
18 Stallage
19 Drawback
21 Crumbs
22 Banner
26 Wasp
27 Cast

70

Across
1 Capricorn
8 Les Misérables
11 Task
12 Frail
13 Topi
16 Courage
17 Example
18 Echidna
20 Picasso
21 Utah
22 Truro
23 Stun
26 Sergeant Major
27 Adversity

Down
2 Arms
3 Reserve
4 Carbine
5 Ruby
6 New South Wales
7 Decomposition
9 Stick 'em up
10 Hidebound
14 Handy
15 Match
19 Acreage
20 Pyrites
24 Aged
25 Taut

71

Across
1 Paratroops
9 Free
10 Self-denial
11 Unison
12 Rapture
15 Perturb
16 Yield
17 Step
18 Visa
19 Seems
21 Matador
22 Berserk
24 Lapped
27 Intolerant
28 Nest
29 Represents

Down
2 Abel
3 Affect
4 Re-entry
5 Ohio
6 Saluted
7 Pressurise
8 Penny Black
12 Resembling
13 Pretty pass
14 Eider
15 Plumb
19 Soldier
20 Seville
23 Scarce
25 Stop
26 Knot

72

Across
1 Come into
5 Auntie
10 Roughly speaking
11 Rattled
12 Riddled
13 Scornful
15 Not on
18 Quest
20 Tardiest
23 Airmail
25 Cabbala
26 Dispassionately
27 Rhymed
28 Crediton

Down
1 Curare
2 Moustache
3 Inhaler
4 Toyed
6 Ugandan
7 Trill
8 Engadine
9 Sparkler
14 Fatalism
16 Testament
17 Squander
19 Teacake
21 Inboard
22 Canyon
24 Raspy
25 Choir

73

Across

7 Cattle pen
8 Paint
10 Optician
11 Angles
12 Peri
13 Negative
15 Peering
17 Haircut
20 Crackpot
22 Slap
25 Harrow
26 Instinct
27 Agree
28 Remission

Down

1 Happy
2 Strife
3 Revision
4 Leaning
5 Laughter
6 Endeavour
9 Fang
14 Rearrange
16 Recorder
18 Assassin
19 Attires
21 Pawn
23 Amidst
24 Actor

74

Across

1 Apart
4 Firmament
8 Racks
9 Youth club
11 Pare
12 Snack
13 Star
16 Argumentative
19 Senior citizen
20 Duck
22 Midas
23 Brie
26 Chameleon
27 Denim
28 Shin-guard
29 Leeds

Down

1 Acropolis
2 Ascertain
3 Test
4 Flying machine
5 Ashy
6 Eclat
7 Tuber
10 Unconstrained
14 Aglow
15 Maize
17 Ignorance
18 Epidermis
20 Decks
21 Coati
24 Berg
25 Idol

75

Across

1 Starting price
10 Quietus
11 Open air
12 Army
13 Pound
14 Blow
17 Hirsute
18 Stilton
19 Antigen
22 Mascara
24 Keep
25 Stink
26 Oral
29 Tessera
30 Italian
31 In confinement

Down

2 Trimmer
3 Rate
4 In store
5 Grounds
6 Rued
7 Chaplet
8 Squash rackets
9 Drawing a blank
15 Purge
16 Rinse
20 Treason
21 Not half
22 Mansion
23 Arraign
27 Hero
28 Palm

76

Across
 1 Doubles up
 8 Eavesdropping
 11 Malta
 12 Rocky
 13 Brass
 16 Uphill
 17 Heroin
 18 Exile
 19 Sevres
 20 Ablest
 21 Spear
 24 Adept
 26 Buffs
 27 Crystal Palace
 28 Cartesian

Down
 2 Omega
 3 Bidder
 4 Exodus
 5 Upper
 6 Walls have ears
 7 Knock-on effect
 9 Ombudsman
 10 Hypnotist
 13 Bless
 14 Alive
 15 Shear
 22 Pedant
 23 Adapts
 25 Tosca
 26 Balsa

77

Across
 1 Air force
 9 Squirrel
 10 Erie
 11 Empty protest
 13 Confuses
 15 Presto
 16 Itch
 17 Snaps
 18 Edam
 20 Inbred
 21 Friendly
 23 Anaesthetist
 26 Haul
 27 Elsinore
 28 Demoniac

Down
 2 In revolt
 3 Free of charge
 4 Rumpus
 5 Espy
 6 Guy-ropes
 7 Arne
 8 Platform
 12 There and then
 14 Staff
 16 Imitates
 17 Sedition
 19 Alleluia
 22 Ibidem
 24 Apse
 25 Eked

78

Across
 1 Take exception to
 9 Waterfowl
 10 Posse
 11 Rehouse
 12 Tel Aviv
 13 Rue
 14 Falsely
 17 Dweller
 19 Thimble
 22 Morpeth
 24 Lea
 25 Elm-tree
 26 Tamable
 28 Get on
 29 Ting-a-ling
 30 Have two left feet

Down
 1 Tower of strength
 2 Ketch
 3 En route
 4 Cookery
 5 Piloted
 6 Impulse
 7 Nashville
 8 One over the eight
 15 Leitmotiv
 16 Lil
 18 Woo
 20 Baronet
 21 Electro
 22 Matinee
 23 Rampart
 27 Brine

79

Across

 1 Islanders
 9 Probate
10 Smash-up
11 Resolve
12 Downright
14 Aswan dam
15 Reveal
17 Satchel
20 Legate
23 Presence
25 Aspirates
26 Exactor
27 Soluble
28 Retinue
29 Riderless

Down

 2 Someone
 3 Absence
 4 Drusilla
 5 Sports
 6 Constable
 7 Ballade
 8 Determine
13 Hatches
15 Raspberry
16 Asserting
18 Elsinore
19 Regatta
21 Gradual
22 Trellis
24 Career

80

Across

 1 Kendal
 4 Spitfire
 9 Invent
10 Snaffles
12 Well
13 Grate
14 Snag
17 Absent-minded
20 Admonishment
23 Away
24 Nitre
25 Rail
28 Teutonic
29 Copita
30 Birdbath
31 Dorset

Down

 1 Knitwear
 2 Novelist
 3 Arno
 5 Penitentiary
 6 Tiff
 7 Island
 8 Ensign
11 Trampolinist
15 Anode
16 Lethe
18 Denarius
19 Stalwart
21 Cantab
22 Valuer
26 Comb
27 Dodo

www.ingramcontent.com/pod-product-compliance
Ingram Content Group UK Ltd.
Pitfield, Milton Keynes, MK11 3LW, UK
UKHW040640280225
455688UK00002B/31